The Process:

Maturity into Sonship, the Prerequisite for Dominion

The Process: Maturity into Sonship, the Prerequisite for Dominion

Lionel Blair, Sr.

Scripture quotations are taken from the King James Version of the Holy Bible unless otherwise marked and is public domain.

Scripture quotations marked CJB from the Complete Jewish Bible by David H. Stern. Copyright © 1998. All rights reserved. Used by permission of Messianic Jewish Publishers, 6120 Day Long Lane, Clarksville, MD 21029. www.messianicjewish.net.

Scripture quotations marked ONMB are taken from the One New Man Bible Copyright © 2011 William J Morford. Used by permission of True Potential Publishing, Inc.

Hebrew and Greek words and definitions are from the Dictionaries of Hebrew and Greek words taken from Strong's Exhaustive Concordance by James Strong, S.T.D., LL.D. 1890 and is public domain.

Excerpts quoted from pg 224, 237 of "The Case for a Creator" © 1952, 2004 by Lee Strobel.

Cover: Designed and Created by Angela Smith

First Printing: 2017

ISBN <978-0-578-19071-6>

Dedication

I want to dedicate this book to my greatest and most loyal friend Jesus Christ. I love you with my entire heart and being. I am nothing without you and you are the reason for my existence. Thank you for loving me unconditionally and showing me such great mercy. I love you forever!

I also want to dedicate this book to all of the leaders and believers alike who are tired of dead religion and who want to truly mature in Christ. I pray this book will drive you to seek the Lord more and position yourself to receive what He paid the price for you to have. With God's grace you can do this.

Contents

Acknowledgements

I would like to acknowledge my lovely wife and co-laborer in ministry Apostle Jasmine Blair. Thank you for believing in me and supporting me. I could not have done this without your continued unconditional love and support.

I would also like to acknowledge all of my spiritual sons and daughters. Your faithfulness to God and the vision He has given me pushes me to be a better husband, father, and leader.

And lastly I would like to thank Apostle Shawn and Prophetess Tora Morris. Thank you for your correction, encouragement, and constant stretching. You all are the best spiritual parents on earth.

Foreword

“The Process" is an apostolic & prophetic treasure trove for your book collection. The author, Apostle Lionel Blair Sr., takes us on a relatable journey into the test, trials, and triumphs of the supernatural process of obtaining the promises of God. There are so many biblical keys that can be found within the chapters of this book, such as: "Self Denial", "Iniquity", "Pride", and "Submission to Authority." Each chapter will prick the characteristic flaws in the mindset of modern-day believers in Christ. Apostle Blair explains in great detail the key components to move and operate in kingdom identity, authority, and power. Also, there are spiritual nuggets in this book entitled: "Ranks & Status", "Kingdom Genetics", "Kingdom Principles of Honor", "Kingdom Faith & The Supernatural", and the "Apostolic & Ekklesia."

I personally know Apostle Blair, and I'm a witness to the fruit and abilities of his ministry and lifestyle. His knowledge of Kingdom protocol and structure supersedes and transcends far beyond his years. As the spiritual father and mentor to Apostle Blair, I have witnessed his ministry go from faith to faith and glory to glory! This man of God lives by his doctrinal beliefs and executes it with class, humility and integrity. His wife, Apostle Jasmine Blair, is also a powerhouse minister of the gospel of Jesus Christ. Together, they govern an apostolic work base in Virginia that extends to many nations abroad.

This written masterpiece will stand the test of time. It will impact generations to come. I believe this book should be apart of the Church’s curriculum across the globe. “The Process" is also a great practice manual for discipleship courses. If you would like to grow and understand the growth development of mentorship and discipleship, then this is the book for you! I am Apostle / Prophet Shawn Morris and I approve this book.

Shawn Morris
President/CEO of Shawn Morris International Ministries
www.shawnmorris.org

Preface

The process! This is a word we do not hear a lot when it comes to ministry preparation or the maturity of the saints in general. As we will discover throughout this book, this will be one of the most important words you will ever hear. We must understand that Jehovah is a God of preparation. He does not call you without any plans to equip you. You cannot go out there all half-cocked and expect to be legitimized in the eyes of the Lord. One thing we must understand is that you can be legitimized by man's standard and not be legitimized by God's standard. One day I was in prayer in my bedroom praying and the Lord appeared to me. He began to teach me about what He called "the law of the process". He began to teach me this simple but powerful revelation. He said to me "everything and everyone that does not go through a process are illegitimate by the standards of the kingdom of God". He also said to me that "everything that has been created went through a time of being formed. A seed starts off small but through a certain measure of time and upkeep, it grows into a tree. Even human life begins in seed form and then grows into a fully developed baby in the womb prior to delivery. No one can escape the process, no one! Everything came from something and everyone came from someone. No one can escape this".

It took me years to write this book. I had to go through many trials and tests before I could even be graced and released to write all that you will read. What I did not mention also was that in this visitation, the Lord Jesus gave me the grace and release to write this book. After years of testing and proving in the many areas that I will discuss with you in this book, the Lord Jesus gave me the green light. So, what is a process exactly? A process is a series of actions or steps taken in order to achieve a particular end. When you look up the definition of the word process, this is what you will find. It is a series of actions, so this means that you can't just do good for one day or do one thing right and expect to arrive. We can't live holy just for one day and expect to get a standing ovation from heaven. This is something that must be walked out daily and you must also increase in this the closer you get to God. And another thing about the process is that you must continue in the things of God and that should yield some type of end results. A seed grows into a tree and that tree yields fruit. The results in the fruit, not the growth of the tree in itself. I find that many people have become prideful in their walk with God because there is evidence of major growth, which is very good, but there's a point where you can no longer grow but now you must produce fruit that others can eat from.

Matthew 21:18,19 "18. Now in the morning as he returned into the city, he hungered. 19. And when he saw a fig tree in the way, he came to it, and found nothing thereon, but leaves only, and said unto it, Let no fruit grow on thee henceforward for ever. And presently the fig tree withered away."

Jesus was hungry, this is why he came to the fig tree to eat. Listen people of God, there are many people who are hungry. They are hungry for more of God. They are tired of dead dry stale religion. They want something fresh from God. When Jesus came to the tree, it showed signs of growth and life but it had no fruit. This is what Jesus do to fruitless ministries and works that are in His name but can't produce anything. We must understand that growth is not a sign of fruit. Life is not a sign of fruit. It's not enough just to have a growing or thriving ministry. These things are great but it's not the main thing God is looking for. There are smaller trees that are able to produce bigger and better quality of fruit than bigger trees. Growth and life are vitally important to get the tree to the place that it can produce fruit but we must realize that the main thing God is looking for the most is the fruit. He's looking for believers, leaders, and ministries to not just grow but to produce fruit. The right word, doctrine, revelation, and presentation will draw people. Nothing is wrong with this but in the midst of all of that, can you demonstrate heaven? The gifts of the Spirit will draw people or cause them to believe but once that is accomplished, can you demonstrate the weight of His glory? Fruit is the end result of a thing, not the thing that caused it to produce or manifest. This is why we must continue and contend for more of God. We are supposed to seek God until we find Him, not glory in the things we pick up along the way.

We must continue along the way knowing that what we are doing and what God is doing in us is preparing us to produce the results that heaven can celebrate. I want to encourage you to never get so caught up in the process and the growth that it produces that you forget the purpose of it all, which is to get you to a place where you can produce actual results. Growth and life is a necessity for fruit to be reproduced but it is not fruit in and of itself. We must always remember that as we stay positioned before God as He processes us to maturity. How do we know that we are producing fruit? We know when we are able to accurately reproduce in others what we have produced as a result of going through God's process of maturity. Leaders hear me well, it's not enough for us to grow and operate in the power of God. We must also be able to reproduce even more powerful people. If your people cannot operate in the same power you operate in and greater then by heaven's standard, you are not producing fruit. In the fruit is more seed. When that seed is picked and planted, it is able to produce another tree that will mature to produce more fruit of its own. If you cannot reproduce what has been produced in you then you are a failure as a leader. As a believer if you cannot help others to get to where you are in God and beyond then you have failed as a believer. You are a fruitless tree whom is on the verge of being cursed.

There comes a time when God comes and visit your tree (personal walk with God, ministry, etc..) and does an inspection. The reason why God causes many to start over is because the original work or tree wasn't fruitful. This is really a work of His mercy. Fruitlessness positions you to receive a curse. This is why you must value the process, submit to the process but also realize that the process has a beginning point and an ending point. There will always be something we will have to learn or receive from God. At the same time there comes a point of time when you are declared mature by the Father. At this place, He then begins to entrusts you with mature things, mature revelation, maturity authority, government, dominion, and the revelation knowledge that comes with these things. We must be proven in order for God to trust us. See, we don't earn God's love, that is freely given. However, we must earn God's trust. Trust must be earned.

The process causes us to earn God's trust. Look at it this way. Would you give someone you barely know or who haven't proven their trustworthiness to you, a key to your house? I would most certainly hope not. That would be very unwise and quite frankly, foolish. So if anyone with any kind of sense would not do that, why do we think that God Himself would do that? When you submit to the process of God for your life, ministry, and destiny, you earn God's trust. You will have no choice but to produce genuine fruit. God is calling us to be fruit producers in this hour. It is time now that we move on to perfection in Him.

Chapter 1

Self Denial: The Work Of The Cross

The Apostle Paul said, "I am crucified with Christ: nevertheless I live; yet not I, but Christ liveth in me: and the life which I now live in the flesh I live by the faith of the Son of God, who loved me, and gave himself for me" (Galatians 2:20). I believe wholeheartedly that this sums up the life of an authentic believer. There are two aspects of our salvation that we will examine before going into the depths of what I will be communicating to you in this book. The first aspect is the forgiveness of sin which deals with the past and what you did; the second is our deliverance from practicing sin which deals with the present and who you are.

The blood of Jesus will wash away your sin, but it cannot wash away your "old man". The old man must be processed out of you. In this book, you will learn how this process works. Most believers only seek forgiveness of their sins. What many call repentance is actually asking God to forgive you of your sins. Some even say that repentance means to turn away from sin; however, neither of these are correct. Repentance means to change your mind or to think differently afterwards; this takes a process. You must understand that confession alone cannot change the nature of a person's heart. Many believe that once their sins are confessed they are in the clear. Yes you may be forgiven, but the problem still remains; what you confessed is still present in your heart. If the nature of who you are currently is not delivered and transformed, then you have the potential to go back to your old ways. This is why many Christians backslide. There is a realm in God, that you can reach, where you don't have to confess your sins everyday. In this realm, your sin nature has no dominion in you or over you. This is where the cross of Jesus comes in.

"Knowing this, that our old man is crucified with him, that the body of sin might be destroyed, that henceforth we should not serve sin" (Romans 6:6). When your old man is crucified then you no longer serve sin; you cannot serve Christ and serve sin. Who or what you serve has dominion over you; the scriptures clearly state that we cannot serve two masters. Either Jesus is your master or sin is your master. Just because you are forgiven of sin doesn't mean that sin isn't in you and that you don't serve it. Forgiveness of sin does not deliver you from the nature of it. The blood of Jesus washes away your sin, but it doesn't wash away your sin nature or your potential to sin. The blood deals with sin, the cross deals with the sinner. Remember that! The cross deals with your fallen nature, the inherited iniquity from Adam passed down to all of humanity. When you get to the place where you are crucified with Christ, sin no longer has dominion in your life and Christ is able to live in you. This is the place where Paul had gotten to and where Galatians 2:20 came from. You cannot truly live by faith until you experience the death of the old man by way of crucifixion. Paul said, "I am crucified with Christ..."(Galatians 2:20); through this death it wasn't him who was alive, but Christ in him. He said, "... I live by the faith of the Son of God..."(Galatians 2:20). You cannot live by faith in the Son of God until you have been crucified with Christ. Until the old man is completely dead, you will always struggle with your faith.

This is bigger than just not sinning. Jesus, God's firstborn, the King of kings, and the Lord of lords, wants to live in and through you; however, you must completely abandon your old nature and receive God's recreated identity for you. I have found throughout my years in ministry that this is one of the most difficult things for believers to do. Instead, we seek ways to justify why we are the way we are. We even seek out teachers who twist scripture to justify the appetites of our old fallen nature in Adam. Nowadays, no one wants to sit under a word or a leader who constantly teaches about our need to die in order to receive all that He is. The modern grace movement tells us that we have this already by faith. If that were true, then we would see more dead people walking around who are truly alive in Christ with absolutely no propensity towards sin whatsoever. We would see more people with absolute loyalty to the kingdom of God apart from humanistic philosophies disguised as "kingdom" teaching. We would see more people operating in the power of God instead of making excuses as to why they don't. Leaders of the twenty-first century have taught God's people how to do everything, except die! I don't agree with everything the old saints did, but one thing I can say is that those leaders took you through a process and made sure you were dead before you were released into ministry. Presently, as long as you have an accurate gift you can be promoted swiftly in ministry. This is not God's way, this is wicked.

God Breaks What is Offered to Him

Man's way of dealing with the old nature and sin is to suppress it; God's way is to remove the sinner altogether. The blood deals with sin, but the cross deals with the iniquity of the old man. The sin nature (not just the sin) is embedded in the old man. What is in Christ cannot sin; however, what is in Adam can and will sin. When we seek to be crucified with Christ it will be a process. The process is designed to get us out of Adam and into Christ (the second or last Adam). Giving ourselves unreservedly to Christ begins this process; during this process many adjustments will be made. God will not allow anything from our old nature to go unaddressed and remain. He will bring the hammer down on everything that is of the old nature in you. "I beseech you therefore, brethren, by the mercies of God, that ye present your bodies a living sacrifice, holy, acceptable unto God, which is your reasonable service"

(Romans 12:1). We are told to present our bodies as a living sacrificeSacrifices are dead when they are offered. Paul said, "I am crucified with Christ: nevertheless I live; yet not I, but Christ liveth in me..." (Galatians 2:20). What am I saying to you? When you die, you also live because He lives in you. That's how you become a living sacrifice. Until then, Christ can never live in you. Jesus became that same living sacrifice on the cross when He died. Just as Jesus was crucified, our old man must also become crucified. God will always break what is offered to Him.

When Jesus blessed the five loaves and the two fishes, the bible says he broke the bread and gave it to His disciples to give to the people. We know that the bread multiplied as He continued to break the bread and give it out (Mark 6:40-42). Jesus is called the bread of life (John 6:35). He is also called the living bread of heaven (John: 6:51). This same bread had to be broken on the cross in order to rule in eternity. Without brokenness there is no rulership. We are supposed to be like the bread that was blessed and broken to be distributed to give life to others. He blessed the bread, then He broke it. The problem with modern day Christianity is that many people want to be blessed, but very few want to be broken. The blessing comes at the place of brokenness. This is the legal way for God to use you to meet the needs of humanity. Jesus' body was broken before He went to the cross. He was broken by the cat of nine tails; the whip that was used to break his skin open. He had to take the chastisement and beating for our sins; he received the chastisement of the Father on our behalf. We have to follow a similar example. We must be broken through the chastisement of the Father in order to be that living bread. To chastise means to correct or discipline. God is not necessarily correcting you for your past sins; they are washed in the blood. God is seeking to correct the way you are by addressing the old man that is currently alive in you. Your old man is the reason why you committed those sins in your past. God is attempting to strip you of Adam's mantle.

Embracing His Chastisement

"I have surely heard Ephraim grieving, 'You have chastised me, and I was chastised, Like an untrained calf; Bring me back that I may be restored, For You are the LORD my God" (Jeremiah 31:18,*ONMB*).

Without chastisement or correction you cannot be restored. Remember... Adam was the first Christ. If Jesus was the second or last Adam then Adam was the first Christ. Until you experience the chastisement of the Lord, you are like an untrained calf who needs to be broken into submission to their masters will. Chastisement brings you to the place of God's original intent. It positions and prepares you to be a habitation for Jesus. Until you submit to the chastisement of the Father, you will always remain untrained. Hear me by the Spirit! I just heard the Lord say, "No matter how learned you are in scripture, in local church life, in protocol knowledge, or in servanthood, by heaven's standard you are untrained until you submit to the process and the chastisement that can only come from me." You will hear more about the chastisement of the Lord as you read this book.

"I will be his father, and he shall be my son. If he commit iniquity, I will chasten him with the rod of men, and with the stripes of the children of men: But my mercy shall not depart away from him, as I took it from Saul, whom I put away before thee" (2 Samuel 7:14,15 KJV).

When you know God as Father you will become acquainted with His discipline. It's different when you know Him as savior or lord. A lord gives orders or commands; lordship deals with God's ownership of you. A lord will address your rebellion, but is not graced to address and reform the depths of your character. A lord will chastise, but a father's chastisement is deeper and more personal. This is why we must learn to accept all the facets of God and not just the parts we are comfortable with. Most Christians have not accepted Him as Lord. They only submit to the savior part of the Father. Many want to be "saved", but very few want to be transformed. God doesn't chastise us for our sins, He chastises us for our iniquities. Even David acknowledged that the source of his transgression was the fact that he had iniquity in him. Iniquity is the inner perverse nature of our old man that we have not yet divorced.

This perversion is not sexual, anything perverse is twisted. Perversion means that something has fallen from its original state and intent; this is the cause of sin. God said that He would chastise us with the rod of men and the stripes of the children of men. What does this mean? God will use other people and situations to expose whatever hidden iniquity is in us. We often suppress things until someone comes along and presses the right button. God will always test and expose you through people. You see... we don't mind being humble secretly before God. It's towards man that we don't want to be humble. We do all that we can to protect our image and reputation before people. It's not until you lose your own reputation that you begin to gain the reputation of God.

You must be willing to lose your reputation with man in order to gain one in the kingdom of God. All of our embarrassment is because of how people view our actions or mistakes. Until you conquer this, you will never be a vessel that God can use. God uses people to deliver you from people. Glory to God! That is good! Only prideful people worry about their reputation. Paul was a good example of this. He was a prominent man among the Sanhedrin and the Jewish people. Once he encountered Jesus and left all of that behind, he began to preach Jesus and the kingdom of God. What he once persecuted, now he is preaching.

He lost respect and admiration among the people of his day, but when Paul abandoned his previous belief system, that's when he began to see the power of God. It took a while for the other apostles to embrace him because of his past, but God even showed up in that! Sometimes God has to make you look bad before people to get you to see the severity of pride of the old man. As you read Paul's writings you can see how he admitted his struggles with the old man and how he overcame it to be crucified with Christ. Many people do not change until they are exposed. Until exposure comes, many do not recognize their need to change because they are blinded by pride. Many times humility comes through humiliation. This is not to belittle you, but to get you to recognize that you need God more than you think.

"Behold, happy is the man whom God correcteth: therefore despise not thou the chastening of the Almighty: For he maketh sore, and bindeth up: he woundeth, and his hands make whole" (Job 5:17,18). We are told not to despise God's chastening. During the chastening process of the Lord, He breaks you and He heals you. You cannot have one without the other and expect to be complete. When God broke Job, he was broken before everyone. There is no such thing as secret brokenness. Jesus never rebuked His disciples privately. He always rebuked them before one another. I have noticed that people behave more when they are corrected openly. For some reason people tend to get their act together when others are watching. I'm not saying all rebukes have to be public,

I just don't see where Jesus had given any private rebukes. When you commit a crime, you come openly before a judge. You don't come in the secret chambers of the judge. There is no such thing as private judgement. When God judges your character He judges it before people. Why is this? I believe that it's bigger than just embarrassment or humiliation to keep us in line... even though I believe these are also strategies of the Father. Sometimes you have to suffer embarrassment in order to be broken; your public brokenness will become your public restoration. God never leaves you broken, remember that! The old nature loves to operate in the secret iniquities in one's life. So exposure is necessary to save your soul!

"And having spoiled principalities and powers, he made a shew of them openly, triumphing over them in it" (Colossians 2:15 KJV).Your embarrassment is not just for you. It's mainly for the enemy working behind the scenes in your life who is using your iniquity that is still present. The enemy doesn't like to be embarrassed. He doesn't want people to see him in a powerless position. If you view it correctly your public rebuke or humiliation is really a place of victory, if you are in will of God. Jesus was humiliated before all, but that was His place of victory. Our victory and salvation came because of His humiliation. We have to change our perspective on how we view our process. Through Jesus' humiliation, the principalities and powers were also humiliated. Through the humility of the Messiah, Satan himself was humbled. This is bigger than you. God is trying to dethrone the enemy from having any placement in your heart and in your life.

"Then I will punish their transgression with the rod and their iniquity with stripes" (Psalms 89:32,*ONMB*). Transgression is rebellion. It's when you do something that you know is wrong, or the opposite of what you have been instructed to do. All of this stems from a structure of iniquity working in you by way of your fallen Adam. We need to learn how to take our rod and our stripes. You must be stripped of the first Adam's garments. This fallen nature has to be weakened through the rod and stripes before you can be completely stripped of it. Our old nature is stubborn.

Breaking Stubbornness

"For rebellion is as the sin of witchcraft, and stubbornness is as iniquity and idolatry..." (1 Samuel 15:23). This says that stubbornness is an iniquity. All rebellion stems from stubbornness; stubbornness always leads to rebellion. Rebellion not relinquished will always result in witchcraft. When one is stubborn, that person is set in their ways. When you address their stubbornness, rebellion will manifest by challenging or questioning what was said, or by refusing to change. This is why stubborn people don't last long in our ministry. Stubborn people, like King Saul, will always lose their inheritance; it is the first step to loss of inheritance. Stubbornness not only makes a person set in their ways, but it also makes a person hard when set in their ways. If a person cannot be persuaded by proven truth, that person has a hardened heart. When submitting to a true process, God begins to address your rebellion by breaking your stubbornness. You cannot be trained until you are broken; major impartation can only take place at the position of brokenness. It takes something hard to break something hard. This is why strong correction and rebukes are necessary for your maturity and development.

Do Not Despise His Chastening

"My son, despise not the chastening of the Lord; neither be weary of his correction: For whom the Lord loveth he correcteth; even as a father the son in whom he delighteth" (Proverbs 3:11,12 KJV).

We are told not to despise this; however, only reason many people despise the chastening of the Lord is because they don't view it properly. Verse 12 tells us that correction is proof of God's love and delight in us. So when God stops correcting and paying attention to you after your refusal to be broken, then you should be concerned. We are also told not to be weary of His correction. Anyone who has been through a real process knows that it can be intense. There will be many times where you feel like you are not doing anything right because you are constantly being addressed and rebuked; it seems like everything you do is under a microscope of scrutiny and criticism. This can make one weary at times. I can remember battling thoughts of giving up, not feeling worthy, not being good enough, or never being able to get it right. All of this was because I didn't understand then what I understand now. It was my faith and obedience that got me through.

I submitted when I didn't understand and I believed God to get me through no matter what! I stood on God's word and promise. This is why I'm in ministry today. Though I didn't despise the chastening of the Lord, I didn't understand it during that time. This is why I had overwhelming thoughts of always disappointing God. But even in that, I submitted anyway and now I have power on my life. Power gained apart from proper processing is witchcraft. I'm not talking about gifts of the Spirit. Those things we receive either from birth or the baptism of the Holy Spirit. I'm talking about the anointing of God. In order for oil to be produced, the olives have to get pressed.

The tool for pressing is something hard not soft. My process showed me how powerless and feeble I was apart from God. It put me in a place of vulnerability and dependency on God. You don't need faith as long as you got it all together (at least in your own mind)! True faith can only work when you recognize your weaknesses and inability to get through whatever you are dealing with without the grace and mercy of God. There's no room for pride and stubbornness when you get to this place. This is how you become crucified with Christ and identify with His death.

When you are dead you have no will and you have no rights. You exchange all of that for His will and His rights. When you truly submit to God you take upon yourself a death sentence. A death sentence is not passed on to the dead, but the living who are about to die. When you are dead you no longer identify with the world. The world no longer has any place in you. You cannot overcome the world by removing yourself from it. Jesus clearly said, "I pray not that thou shouldest take them out of the world, but that thou shouldest keep them from the evil" (John 17:15 KJV). So God is not trying to take us out of the world, He is trying to take the world out of us. You cannot change a system that has gripped your heart. There was a time when the church rejected the ways of the world. Now, the church uses worldly ways and methods to draw crowds and keep people comfortable. This is why the church is getting richer, but is decreasing in power. The process is so important. We must get back to consecration.

Chosen Among the Chosen

In the old testament there were three classes among God's people: The nation of Israel as a whole, the Levites, and Aaron and his sons which made up the priesthood. Israel saw and experienced the glory from afar, the Levites worked within close proximity of the glory, and the priest had closer contact and direct access to the glory. When God first brought Israel out of Egypt, He told them that He was going to make them a kingdom of priests and a holy nation (Exodus 19:6 KJV). God's intention from the beginning was to have a kingdom of people who would all know Him in a special way and be close to Him; however, their faithfulness was tested when Moses went to the mountain to receive the commandments. Moses took too long for their comfort and so they decided to make a golden calf to conjure up the Egyptian gods that God used Moses to deliver them from. Once their sin was discovered, Moses asked who was on the Lord's side.

The Levites immediately stepped forward and proved that they were on the Lord's side. Later, God chose to strip all of Israel of the priesthood rank, responsibility, and relationship, and gave it to the tribe of Levi and the sons of Aaron. When you choose not to go along with all of what everyone else is doing to uphold the original standard of God, then He will separate you from the rest. One of the major problems I see with the church today is most of the church goes along with anything the world popularizes. They adopt it into their customs and worship God. This is why very few people carry the glory today. We have many gifted people on the scene, but they have no glory on their lives. When you die to yourself you are also dead to the world. You don't accept the customs and culture of the world. You cannot make an impact by conforming, you only make an impact by standing out.

Another thing about the Levites... they had the greatest and most tangible relationship with God in the Old Testament, but they were the biggest servants and they were rarely seen. When you are separated by God unto God, the first thing that goes is your visibility to others. God strips you of the honor and recognition of man and you take upon yourself His honor in secrecy and separation. Those who served in the sanctuary were rarely seen by men. They were seen by God all the time, but they were separated so that man couldn't see them on a regular basis. The Levites were servants of the temple. They did everything within the secrecy of God's glory. They never received any glory or praise from men. Until you go through this period as a believer your consecration will be incomplete. The cross separates you and crucifies you. Satan's defeat was at the cross. The only way to defeat the enemy in your life is by crucifying yourself with Christ.

Calvary is the Way to Pentecost

There is no resurrection without the crucifixion. "That I may know him, and the power of his resurrection, and the fellowship of his sufferings, being made conformable unto his death" (Philippians 3:10). You cannot know Him in the power of His resurrection without embracing the fellowship of His suffering. There's no glory without the gory. There is no shortcut or substitute for this. You cannot have one without the other; Calvary paved the way for Pentecost. The crucifixion of Jesus made the outpouring at Pentecost possible. This is also what's wrong with the church today.

They are seeking and asking God for an outpouring while they are still alive and governed by their old man. The first Adam lost the glory and dominion by becoming a lesser being. The last Adam recovered the glory and dominion that was lost by dying on the cross and being resurrected into a greater being. There is no glory without suffering and death. "For I reckon that the sufferings of this present time are not worthy to be compared with the glory which shall be revealed in us" (Romans 8:18). Glory cannot be revealed until there's a suffering and sacrifice of death. You cannot ask for glory, but not be willing to embrace the suffering.

Gethsemane, the Way to Calvary (The Cross)

Before we can be obedient at Calvary, we must come to the place of obedience at Gethsemane. Gethsemane means olive press, or a press of oils, in the Greek and Hebrew. This is the place where your will dies. Before your old man dies, your will to stay alive in it has to die. This is the place where you allow God to press on you so much and so intensively that you surrender your complete will to Him. His will is that you die to everything outside of the kingdom so that you can receive His glory upon your life. Gethsemane is the place where God presses on your will until you give in to His will. In this place, your will dies so that His will can be lived out through you. His will is for you to be crucified with Christ so that Christ can live in and through you. This is not just accomplished by faith like so many teach. This is accomplished by death and complete surrender. Gethsemane is the place where God sets you apart and consecrates you for death. You cannot be completely led by the Spirit of God to become a son of God unless you submit to Gethsemane and Calvary. Until then, you are not Spirit led. You cannot be dead to the flesh while being alive in the old man.

In the place of Gethsemane, the will of your soul and spirit is divided (Hebrews 4:12). Your will is embedded in the soulish part of your being. Jesus said that in this place the spirit is willing, but the flesh is weak (Matthew 26:41). Your flesh is also part of your soulish man that is not surrendered to God. This is what governs the body to sin against God. Your will and your flesh are all soulish. We need the word of God to separate the two. After a separation, or distinguishing between the two, can you identify the base nature of your flesh and make it subject to what God is doing in your spirit. The spirit is always willing to obey God, but the old man embedded in the soulish man fights it.

"This I say then, Walk in the Spirit, and ye shall not fulfil the lust of the flesh. For the flesh lusteth against the Spirit, and the Spirit against the flesh: and these are contrary the one to the other: so that ye cannot do the things that ye would" (Galatians 5:16,17 KJV).

Your flesh does not want to surrender, it does not want to die. Your flesh is your old nature and it doesn't want to lose it's place of dominance in your life. You must aggressively fight your old man and strip yourself of Adam's mantle so that you can receive the mantle of Christ. There is something in you that is fighting you. Your flesh and the old man is stubborn. Gethsemane is the place where God breaks your stubbornness. In order to prevail you must fight back by not only rebuking it, but also by completely surrendering your self governance to God and His pressure. Our will is so stubborn under the old man that God has to apply pressure to break it. We must be broken and dead in order to be completely used by God.

This is why separation of soul and spirit is important. We need words like this to show us what is soulish and what is spiritual. This is also why we submit to the judgements of the Lord for our life; judgment comes to distinguish. In this place you really get to know yourself (Deuteronomy 8 KJV). God's aim is to lead you to the end of yourself so that you may know your true self. Struggle and opposition reveal your character; it reveals what you have in you. The longer you cling to yourself, the longer you will stay in the wilderness to be pressed. You will experience more and more defeat. When God orchestrates your defeat, it's always for the purpose of exposing your true self and the old man that's still alive. Until you conquer yourself and die, you will never mature. Maturity begins where you (the old man) ends. True grace empowers us to end ourselves and to begin completely in Christ. This is what the process is all about.

Chapter 2
Our Original Design in the Kingdom of God

The purpose of this book is to teach about God's process of maturity and to illustrate what has been made available to those committed to maturity in their walk with the Lord. In the kingdom of God, there is a specific way the Father has ordained things to be. We cannot change or vote against these things simply because we do not agree. Before we go any further... What is the kingdom? It is the domain of a king, where the king rules, and where God's will is accepted and enforced as law. It's where the King's thoughts and ideas shape everyday culture. Wherever God rules, that is where His kingdom exists! The kingdom of God is the central theme of scripture. Even though the term wasn't mentioned in the writings of the old testament, the reality or truth concerning it was present. Israel was a visible representation of God's invisible kingdom on earth. God originally designed man to live in a kingdom structure and culture.

"And God said, Let us make man in our image, after our likeness: and let them have dominion over the fish of the sea, and over the fowl of the air, and over the cattle, and over all the earth, and over every creeping thing that creepeth upon the earth. So God created man in his own image, in the image of God created he him; male and female created he them. And God blessed them, and God said unto them, Be fruitful, and multiply, and replenish the earth, and subdue it: and have dominion over the fish of the sea, and over the fowl of the air, and over every living thing that moveth upon the earth" (Genesis 1:26-28).

We must understand kingdom terminology; language constitutes the culture of a society, nation, or a kingdom. Let's explore the word "dominion" in this passage of scripture. The Hebrew word is "radah" which means: to rule, dominate, and subjugate (bring under control or domination, to make someone or something subordinate to). Being afraid of dominion will prevent the Church from experiencing the reality of it. Our original design was to function in a kingdom, not a religious institution. Adam and Eve were created to function like God with power, authority, and dominion to govern and dominate all in the earth. Now... let me point something out to you. When God created man in His image, He created them as full grown adults: not infants, not toddlers, not teenagers, but adults. This was because He could not give mature authority and power to an immature creation; Adam and Eve were made mature. Now because of our fallen nature, we have to submit to God's true process of maturity. The model for maturity in God is to rise to the stature of the fullness of Christ. Remember... Jesus was the second Adam which made Adam the first Christ. His likeness comes with His processing into maturity. Until you are mature, you will never fully be Christlike nor will God entrust you with His power.

Adam and Eve were supposed to rule the earth just like God ruled heaven and their reality was supposed to spread from the garden of Eden to all of the known world. God's mandate for man has not changed; we still have that same commission today. We are to advance God's kingdom until it consumes and dominates the whole earth! Do you think God would have entrusted such a valuable mission to a baby? Mature assignments are given when your stature in God is mature. Our experience with God is our message to man. We're called to spread it like wildfire! We must know how to properly enter the kingdom in order to spread it's culture, influence, and dominance throughout the world. This is why God told Adam and Eve to multiply their seed, fill the earth, and subdue it. I will cover more details on this topic later. In the garden of Eden, the kingdom of God was established on the earth; it's borders were in need of expansion until it filled the earth. Remember... the earth was without form and void. Many scholars believe that this described the fall of Lucifer because God doesn't make anything formless or void and I hold this same belief. We can see where the Spirit of God began to restore the earth and create the environment for Adam and Eve to prosper. True prosperity in the kingdom of God is linked to and enclosed in the Holy Spirit. Anything outside of that has its origins from another kingdom.

Kick The Devil Off The Planet

I strongly believe that Adam and Eve's original mandate was to kick the devil off the planet by spreading the Kingdom's culture all throughout the earth. The fallen angel, Lucifer, and other fallen angels were roaming the earth during that time. Due to these unwanted guests trying to establish a demonic kingdom, Adam an Eve had to subdue the earth. God's original intent for us was similar... to rule and smother Earth with His kingdom culture! The Church is trying to escape from the devil, but the reality is he should be trying to escape from us. We have embraced the doctrines of demons that promotes defeat and pessimism in the body of Christ. We are waiting on Jesus to rescue us when He has given us the authority and power to change the world; this is cowardice in heart.

One thing I have learned about God is this: He will never do for us what we have the ability to do or what He has commanded us to do for ourselves. When you become more mature in God this becomes more of a reality in your understanding. It's time that we change our paradigm of thinking and be the rulers God has designed us to be! Maturity positions you to rule.

The Blessing

"And when Abram was ninety years old and nine, the Lord appeared to Abram, and said unto him, I am the Almighty God; walk before me, and be thou perfect. And I will make my covenant between me and thee, and will multiply thee exceedingly. And Abram fell on his face: and God talked with him, saying, As for me, behold, my covenant is with thee, and thou shalt be a father of many nations. Neither shall thy name any more be called Abram, but thy name shall be Abraham; for a father of many nations have I made thee. And I will make thee exceeding fruitful, and I will make nations of thee, and kings shall come out of thee. And I will establish my covenant between me and thee and thy seed after thee in their generations for an everlasting covenant, to be a God unto thee, and to thy seed after thee" (Genesis 17:1-7).

We are the seed of Abraham by faith (Galatians 3:28,29; Romans 9:6-8). God promised Abraham that he would be the father of royalty. By faith, we are partakers of the royal lineage and covenant that God made with him. God appeared to Abram when he was 99 years old; He waited until he was a seasoned veteran in the kingdom to make this covenant with him. Maturity positions you for greater covenant promises with God; it maximizes this covenant in our lives. Even though many of us are immature, we are still partakers of this covenant promise. This was confirmed when God made the same promise to Jacob, Abraham's grandson.

"And God appeared unto Jacob again, when he came out of Padanaram, and blessed him. And God said unto him, Thy name is Jacob: thy name shall not be called any more Jacob, but Israel shall be thy name: and he called his name

Israel. And God said unto him, I am God Almighty: be fruitful and multiply; a nation and a company of nations shall be of thee, and kings shall come out of thy loins" (Genesis 35:9-11).

The blessing of God is linked to rulership and kings. In Genesis 17:16, God told Abraham that He was going to bless Sarah, his wife, to be a mother of nations and kings. In Genesis 1:28, God blessed Adam and Eve prior to them being instructed to subdue the earth. To function in God's kingdom by original design, you must first become a recipient of the blessing of God. What does it mean to be blessed by God? The Hebrew word for blessed is "barak", which means: to be adorned, to kneel, to praise, and to salute. Holy Spirit spoke to me concerning this definition and said, "These words are expressions of honor." To be blessed by God means to be honored by God.

The only way to be honored by God is to first honor God. "...for them that honour me I will honour, and they that despise me shall be lightly esteemed" (1 Samuel 2:30). Salvation is free, but honor is earned; however, we must seek the honor that comes from God, not man. Even the devil has to respect the honor bestowed on us by God! I will touch on this in greater detail later; however, great honor comes from God when you have endured the process. Everyone deserves honor, but as we will see later on, there are different levels of it. The higher levels will only come when you are mature enough to handle it. I need you to understand that the blessing of the Lord was never intended for you to acquire a bunch of "stuff". The blessing was given so that we can rule as kings and princes in the kingdom of God. Honor also means to highly esteem. When you are honored by the Lord, you are highly esteemed by Him; kings and princes are highly esteemed.

The Father's Good Pleasure

As previously stated, God's will was for His people to rule this planet. As the kingdom continues to advance on the earth, everything that exists should eventually be subdued by the people of God. It is imperative for us to embrace this mindset if we're going to live and operate according to our original design; however, man has a history of losing the kingdom. In Luke 12:32, Jesus said that it's the Father's good pleasure to give us the kingdom. It's the Father's good pleasure to give us His dominion and our own dominion. We are called to rule in this life! Why is it that we don't have it? I believe it's because many of us have submitted to another kingdom order. That is what Adam and Eve did when they entertained the suggestion of the serpent and acted on it. Jesus came to take the imperial crown from Satan which Adam forfeited as a result of his rebellion.

After His death, burial, and resurrection, Jesus was able say that all power and authority have been given unto Him in heaven and in earth. This is the same authority Christ shares with His Ekklesia. In Exodus 19:1-6, God delivered Israel out of Egypt, He tried to establish the kingdom among them; however, they did not receive the fullness of it because of fear and unbelief. This was demonstrated in their murmuring and complaining against Moses. We are supposed to be a kingdom of priests, a royal dominion of people, who have access to God and are able to demonstrate and manifest the realities of His original intent for the world.

The Ekklesia

"But ye are a chosen generation, a royal priesthood, an holy nation, a peculiar people; that ye should shew forth the praises of him who hath called you out of darkness into his marvellous light" (1 Peter 2:9 KJV). The people of God were originally intended to be a kingdom of governmental people; a similar scripture is quoted in Exodus 10:6. God's original design for us is to become a kingdom of royal priests. We are called to be priests who understand royalty and operate in royal power, authority, and rank. Sadly, most of the Church today is operating beneath this standard, but all of that is about to change in the years to come! God is taking us back to His original design so that we can move forward in the proper understanding of our role in advancing His kingdom.

"When Jesus came into the coasts of Caesarea Philippi, he asked his disciples, saying, Whom do men say that I the Son of man am? And they said, Some say that thou art John the Baptist: some, Elias; and others, Jeremias, or one of the prophets. He saith unto them, But whom say ye that I am? And Simon Peter answered and said, Thou art the Christ, the Son of the living God. And Jesus answered and said unto him, Blessed art thou, Simon Barjona: for flesh and blood hath not revealed it unto thee, but my Father which is in heaven. And I say also unto thee, That thou art Peter, and upon this rock I will build my church; and the gates of hell shall not prevail against it. And I will give unto thee the keys of the kingdom of heaven: and whatsoever thou shalt bind on earth shall be bound in heaven: and whatsoever thou shalt loose on earth shall be loosed in heaven. Then charged he his disciples that they should tell no man that he was Jesus the Christ" (Matthew 16:13-20).

All of this took place at Caesarea Philippi. This is very important! In Greek, the word church is the word "ekklesia", which means something totally different from what we've come to know today. Further research will prove that word "church" was not in the original Greek text of the new testament. It was placed there on the authority of King James for political reasons. King James authorized the translation of the scriptures from Aramaic, Hebrew, and Greek to English. Why did Jesus say that He will build His ekklesia? They were in Caesarea Philippi which was a Greek city state under the Roman Empire. Their form of government was called the

Ekklesia. This government was formed by elected elders who had gone to war and had multiple years of experience. In other words, they were mature. Again, it goes back to maturity and they were experienced in war and government. Babies should never be in government, period. The elders would meet at the gates of the city to deliberate on judicial issues regarding the communities of which they presided.

Now take everything I just stated and spiritualize it. You will see the true purpose of the Ekklesia. The Greek word "ekklesia" is made from two words: "Ekk" means to be called out FROM a source of authority and "caleo" means to call out or SPEAK FROM a source of authority. Being called out from a source of authority is directly related to being separated for the governmental use of the Father. Speaking from a source of authority refers to the delegated authority invested in those set apart to make laws through verbal decrees. When you possess the approval and the vested authority of the Father, your words carry a heavier weight in the spirit realm. As Christ's ekklesia, we are called and set apart by Him to rule in the gates of our cities, communities, or anywhere that we have been assigned to; this is for control of the spiritual climate in that jurisdiction. Those who possess the gates control what goes in, what goes out, and what is permitted. This was originally an apostolic mandate and function, but the apostles are also to mobilize people to assist with this task. We must allow the Lord to mature us so that we can possess the gates of our assigned location and to maintain kingdom governance there. Without maturity God will never entrust you with this kind of authority.

We were never designed to come together just for praise, worship, and the word only. This is what religion has reduced us to! We are used to governing a building and the activities within it, but no one is really governing the kingdom. Also, we were supposed to come together to dictate the spiritual climate of our cities and regions and charged with the spiritual maintenance of that territory. Please note: the Ekklesia were elders who gathered at the gates. Eldership in this context denotes spiritual maturity. The Ekklesia should be a mature body of believers, under apostolic authority, whom the Lord can trust with delegated authority to govern. It is illegal in the kingdom for babies and children to be in government!

We are supposed to be a government on the earth that is authorized by God to determine and proclaim edicts and judicial laws of heaven; the Ekklesia are the congressmen of the kingdom of God. We gather together to identify the issues concerning the kingdom and our assigned territory. Our decrees become spiritual laws that the angels of God execute and enforce. Heaven backs the Ekklesia! We sit at the portals of our city and determine what will be allowed in our city. Remember....this is only for those who are mature in Christ.

We are called to be more than just Sunday morning pew warmers! There is a power available to us that we have not tapped into. Though it's available for us, there is a process that we must allow God to take us through. We will not only deduce the fullness of this power, but also possess the maturity to maintain it without being destroyed. We will discover all of this and more in this book. Our original design in the kingdom of God is dominion and rulership. Many fail to point out that in the beginning, God gave that dominion and rulership to a grown (mature) Adam and Eve. You must be fully committed to maturity to get the full birthright. The inheritance is only given when you are ready. You must be committed to maturity!

Chapter 3
The Ekklesia of the Kingdom

Christ's vision for the Ekklesia was governmental in origin. This is the ancient function that is being restored to the Church. Without our governmental function, we cannot say that we're truly the Ekklesia. If we remain babes in Christ and children in God during our entire walk with the Lord, then we cannot say we are the Ekklesia. Every church that is truly called by God has a divine responsibility where they are planted. When I say "church" I'm not talking about a building, I'm talking about mature people who understand the government of the kingdom of God. I'm talking about Christ's Ekklesia. Every one of us has a role in God's government to advance His kingdom in the areas that we have been assigned. Previously, I stated how the Ekklesia would sit at the gates of the city and make decrees and laws concerning their region. We hear a lot about "gatekeeping churches", but only a matured apostolic assembly of believers that has been established by God will be charged to watch these gates. According to the scriptures, the Ekklesias were established by mature apostolic leaders who placed elders (matured leaders) in place to govern. It's not enough just to say you have a church! Does your church serve a governmental role and purpose for the kingdom of God in your city? How many churches in our cities actually belong to God or were established correctly?

Power and Authority

Proof that we belong to God will be seen in how we function. How you function will tell who's offspring you really are and the origins of where you come from. Functionality can also be genetic; anything genetic deals with generation. The word "gene" can be seen in both words. The original church not only had power, but they also had authority. Power allows you to demonstrate the existence or the reality of the kingdom. Authority gives you the right to rule and allows you to enforce the laws of the kingdom for your region or wherever you have been assigned. When you have power you enforce the law. When you have authority you make the law. What is enforced in the spiritual realm will be demonstrated in our natural world. Ultimately, this should open doors for believers to be placed in positions of influence in government, business, etc., so that we can start seeing the natural change we are so diligently prophesying and praying for. The Ekklesia are people of power and authority who decide what is lawful in our region. What is allowed is because we allow it. Sadly, much of the Church is impressed by power and gifts, but authority is hard to recognize. Authority will cause demons to respect you and obey your commands!

"And God wrought special miracles by the hands of Paul: So that from his body were brought unto the sick handkerchiefs or aprons, and the diseases departed from them, and the evil spirits went out of them. Then certain of the vagabond Jews, exorcists, took upon them to call over them which had evil spirits the name of the Lord Jesus, saying, We adjure you by Jesus whom Paul preacheth. And there were seven sons of one Sceva, a Jew, and chief of the priests, which did so. And the evil spirit answered and said, Jesus I know, and Paul I know; but who are ye? And the man in whom the evil spirit was leaped on them, and overcame them, and prevailed against them, so that they fled out of that house naked and wounded" (Acts 19:11-16).

In this passage of scripture, Apostle Paul demonstrated both power and authority by healing the sick and casting out demons. True authority is shown in our ability to expel the demonic nationally, regionally, territorially, or individually. How is it that we gain authority? We gain or receive authority through revelation. Before any man or woman of God can receive divine authority, they must first begin to receive revelation from God. I'm not talking about reading revelation that another man wrote. I'm talking about personal revelation through a personal encounter with the Lord. This is what happened to the Apostle Peter in Matthew 16 when he caught the revelation of who Jesus was as the Christ (anointed to rule) and the Son of the living God. Because of this, he received the keys of the kingdom. Divine revelation will make heaven a right now reality, but this only comes through true intimacy with God. Authority without intimacy is false authority. If we are the true Ekklesia, then we must get back to intimacy with the Father. You can't ride on someone else's revelation and think you have authority. You must have your own relationship even if God shows you something similar to what He has revealed to others. Again, you cannot ride on someone else's revelation!

This is what the seven sons of Sceva did. They tried to grasp Paul's revelation without any personal relationship with God or submission to any type of spiritual authority. Even though we can glean from the revelation of others, we still must go through our own intimacy to access the revelation and authority we need. This is why the demon possessed man was able to overpower them; they were addressing a prince demon of a city with false authority. If you are not submitted to authority then you have no authority. The Ekklesia are people who understand and value the sovereign authority of God and His vested authority in others. As I am writing this the Lord spoke to me and said, "You will never fully mature without being submitted to authority." The Church must grasp this... Especially emerging and currently functioning apostolic and prophetic leaders.

Bringing Order Out of Chaos

In Acts 19, we see another example of how the Church is supposed to be. The Apostle Paul caused quite a stir in Ephesus and throughout Asia. Paul's ministry put a dent in the businesses that benefited from the worship of the false god Diana. The people of the city came together in an unsanctioned meeting to accuse the Apostle Paul's ministry. When the town clerk stood up to set order to the meeting, he told the accusers that they needed to handle their disputes in a lawful assembly. If this clerk was a believer in the kingdom of God, then he did exactly what we should be doing as the Ekklesia. The Apostle Paul caused this principality operating through the worship of Diana to lose much ground through his ministry. Let me remind you that Paul's ministry was supernatural in nature. If we as believers don't embrace the supernatural, then we won't be able to do much damage to the kingdom of darkness. The scriptures tell us that death reigned from Adam to Moses. Why did it stop at Moses? Because Moses had unusual supernatural powers and authority from God that no one else had before him. He delivered a whole nation from slavery through the supernatural! Through the supernatural, Paul also demonstrated how powerless Diana was in comparison to the kingdom of God.

The town clerk set order to the chaos during this unlawful assembly. We as the Ekklesia are called to bring order to chaos and to disband unlawful demonic assemblies. Also, there are some assemblies today that are unlawful and not sanctioned by God or approved by a higher authority. By kingdom standards, many churches today are unlawful and illegal in the spirit. God is strategic in what He does! He doesn't need a lot of churches in one city. The only ones needed are those who He has ordained to understand who they are and what they have been called to do. It's time to stop having church and start being the church! To go back to the town clerk... What he did in Ephesus is what we should be doing in our region. In this context a town clerk is described as a writer, scribe which is used in Acts 19:35 of a state clerk, an important official, variously designated, according to inscriptions found in Graeco-Asiatic cities. He was responsible for the form of decrees first approved by the Senate, then sent for approval in the popular assembly in which he presided.

In the spirit we are supposed to preside over cities, workplaces, etc. According to the laws of the kingdom we declare what will be and what will not be permitted. As the Ekklesia, we make declarations in alignment with the royal laws of heaven to make laws here on earth by decreeing those things into manifestation. We also make decrees and laws that heaven is in agreement with. This will make it easier for believers to occupy positions of influence in the world so that the kingdom of God can be enforced and experienced in all the other places of influence. It's sad how secular institutions and civil government can grasp kingdom principles better than us. The word "ekklesia" was originally a political word. Jesus said, "Upon this rock I will build my church..." In other words, my congressman, royal officials, and the officials that will help me govern my Father's empire on the earth. I hope you are starting to get a picture of who we are called to be.

The gates of hell will not prevail against the Ekklesia.... Why? By giving the keys of the kingdom to senior apostolic government, we can shut the gates of hell, stand in the gates of our cities, and open them up for the King of glory and His kingdom to close all access to demonic infiltration. Now, even though there was a special set of keys given to Peter, I believe that the Ekklesia are given kingdom keys of authority too. It may not be the same set the Apostle Peter had, but we are given our spe keys to open and shut doors that God wills us too. Every true apostle has a set of keys to shut the gates of hell against the government of God. This is how we will establish order in chaos. The problem is that we have allowed satan's ekklesia to sit at the gates of our cities and regions, making their own laws and decrees. We will not stand for this any longer!

The Importance of Maturity in Governance

In Rome, you had to be at least 50 to 60 years old to be elected to the Roman Senate; by that time you would have gained enough wisdom and experience. You had to know what it was like to go to war, conquer territories, and govern them before you could be entrusted to manage the Roman empire. Galatians 4:4 says that Jesus came in the "fullness of time." I believe the fullness of time was when Rome came into power. Rome had the perfect model and system of governance, but had wicked leadership. It's very possible to have a perfect system of leadership or governance and have wicked leaders occupying seats of authority.

You had to be mature with experience to occupy an office in Rome. I find it quite silly that people want high positions of authority, but they can't conquer their own personal devils. We all should be maturing and progressing to perfection, not going around the same circle with the same devils. You have to be experienced in God in order to govern. Hear me in the spirit! This has nothing to do with age, but spiritual maturity. Experience and maturity had to do with your age in Rome, but in the spirit it is not always so. You have to be mature to qualify for governance. Babes in Christ can display the power of the kingdom, but authority to rule and to govern are given to those who have submitted to the processing of the Father for maturity.

"For the earnest expectation of the creature waiteth for the manifestation of the sons of God. For the creature was made subject to vanity, not willingly, but by reason of him who hath subjected the same in hope, Because the creature itself also shall be delivered from the bondage of corruption into the glorious liberty of the children of God. For we know that the whole creation groaneth and travaileth in pain together until now" (Romans 8:19-22).

Sonship always denotes maturity. When mature believers are established in a region, everything there should come into divine alignment to serve the purposes of God's kingdom. Even creation lines up when sons are manifested! All of creation was subject to the fall of Adam but now that Christ has removed the curse, the sons of God have been given the mandate of restoring the earth and reforming it back to God's original intent. His original intent will bring better promises under Christ Jesus. Sons manifest kingdom government in the earth. They have authority because they have history and experience with God. True sons are current with God because they know Him intimately and are mature enough to understand government. As long as you resist, despise, or don't understand government, you are still a babe or child in God (no matter how old you are). Jehovah will not entrust governmental rank, authority, and responsibility to babes; they are not mature enough to handle such weight and would be crushed under it.

"Now I say, That the heir, as long as he is a child, differeth nothing from a servant, though he be lord of all; But is under tutors and governors until the time appointed of the father. Even so we, when we were children, were in bondage under the elements of the world: But when the fulness of the time was come, God sent forth his Son, made of a woman, made under the law, To redeem them that were under the law, that we might receive the adoption of sons. And because ye are sons, God hath sent forth the Spirit of his Son into your hearts, crying, Abba, Father. Wherefore thou art no more a servant, but a son; and if a son, then an heir of God through Christ" (Galatians 1:1-7).

As long as you remain a babe or a child you will not inherit the full authority to govern in God's kingdom. You will constantly need tutors and governors (spiritual leaders) to teach you about the kingdom and how to govern. Once you have reached maturity the only thing needed after that is oversight to keep you accountable; strict instruction and command of leadership is also not needed. Our assemblies are supposed to be full of people who are maturing into sons of God so that they can take their proper place in the government of God in the earth. This is the birthright of the Church and is part of our inheritance! The kingdom of darkness is constantly fighting us so that we will not come into our full inheritance as matured sons and joint heirs with Christ. Until you reach this place you are not a part of the Ekklesia. The true Ekklesia will consist of mature sons of God who are able to be trusted with the responsibility of governance in God's kingdom. I'm not saying you don't belong to God... I am saying that you are not a part of His Ekklesia, His government in the earth. Stay with me on this! I will teach more in depth about the Ekklesia in the next chapter. I am laying a foundation for our identity and who we are supposed to become before I get into the meat of what this book is about. If you are not mature or committed to maturity and processing then you are not apart of the Ekklesia.

Chapter 4
Apostleship and the Ekklesia

There are many apostles in the twenty-first century who are caught up in their apostleship and have neglected to execute the original mandate of their existence and functionality. Many assume the title “apostle”, but are not apostles in function. This is another reason why I cannot mention the process enough. Going through the process of maturation will ensure you a title, but most importantly you will have the power and authority of the office. I find that many do not have the basic understanding of why Jesus instituted the apostleship from the beginning. This generation of apostolic leaders must become apostles not only by title, but most importantly by function! We live in a generation of what I call "title grabbers."

Whatever is popular in mainstream Christianity is what people grab on to. I can remember when God started bringing the office of the prophet back into the Body of Christ. Everyone started running around saying they are a prophet! No proof of process, just a gift. It is the same thing with the apostleship. I believe this is a season where the Lord Himself will prove those who are authentically His. Apostleship is supposed to be tried and proven. "..... thou hast tried them which say they are apostles, and are not, and hast found them liars" (Revelation 2:2 KJV). Those who carry the title of apostle, but do not exhibit the apostleship function and fruit are liars according to the word of God.

The Ancient Function Of The Apostle

First of all lets look at the meaning of the word "apostle." In Greek, it is the word “apostolos” which is defined as: one that is sent, a special messenger, a delegate, an envoy (messenger or representative especially one on a diplomatic mission), and one sent with the power of attorney. Apostolos was originally a secular Greek term that was used by Greeks and Romans that described special envoys that were sent out to establish the dominion of the empire. It is not a religious word, but a governmental word to describe the delegates in authority and power to establish the continuum of the empire's dominion. We cannot limit the apostolic to the Church because it's origins are outside of the Church; Jesus established the apostleship before He established the Church.

During the classical Greek and Roman eras the word "apostolos" referred to: someone who was the commander of a naval expedition, a cargo, or a fleet of ships sent out on special missions. The apostolos were commanders or admirals of the naval expedition or the fleet of ships. They were given charge to subdue and conquer territories through the threat of military might. A true apostolos is always advancing into the new. After these territories were subdued they were charged to train and convert the new subjects to the culture of the empire. The first thing they did was tear down the old government and establish a new government.

They took the people that were loyal to Rome (e.g., ex-Roman soldiers living in the city or the elders of the land that were willing to convert to Roman culture) and established them as the fathers or elder brothers and city council. This is also how the apostles established the Ekklesia during that time; they went into a region, tore down the old government, and established a new government (a.k.a. the Ekklesia). Apostles have the ability to identify mature sons and ordain them in positions of governance. This is why they chose the elders of the city and those who had experience in war to help govern the newly conquered territory. Apostles only deal in the realm of maturity. If you are not committed to maturity then you are going to find it extremely difficult to walk with a true apostle. It is also the apostle that places a demand on your life to mature into your sonship with the Father.

The entire concept of apostleship is this: to be sent out with orders to subdue, conquer, convert, and to culturize. They are sent with full power and authority of the empire (the Kingdom of God) to accomplish this. A Hebrew word synonymous with apostolos is the word “shaliach”. The shaliach was a legal institution in Rabbinic Judaism established to ensure that an appointed messenger was given due regard as the legal representative of his sender and functioned with the full authority of the one who commissioned him. In Jewish tradition, a man’s agent (shaliach) is acting as the man himself. The shaliach not only acted in place of his sender, but he also acted as the sender. This is very important to understand!

The shaliach had a function that was more legal than religious; they served documents, collected money, carried information, etc. “Come now therefore, and I will send thee unto Pharaoh, that thou mayest bring forth my people the children of Israel out of Egypt” (Exodus 3:10). Moses was God’s shaliach. The word “send” in that passage is the word "shaliach" in Hebrew. “Also I heard the voice of the Lord, saying, Whom shall I send, and who will go for us? Then said I, Here am I; send me" (Isaiah 6:8 KJV). Isaiah was also God’s shaliach. There are many old testament prophets who functioned in this apostolic dimension. If they were in the new testament, they would be apostles.

The basic function of the apostleship is military and ambassadorial in nature. They embody the authority and the culture of the kingdom (God's empire). This is why true apostles must have an accurate understanding of the kingdom of God. Today, most professed apostles understand ecclesiastical protocols and how to dress like Roman Catholics, but they do not accurately understand the kingdom of God. To be an authentic apostle, you must have accurate understanding of the kingdom of God! The disciples spent 3½ years being taught by Jesus about the kingdom before they were released into the full functionality of their apostleship.

Though Jesus called them apostles in Matthew 10, their sphere of governance was limited. Until they were fully released, they were only allowed to function partially in their apostleship and were limited to the house of Israel. When they were released into the fullness of their apostleship, that's when they started engaging and dethroning principalities, delivering cities, and turning the world upside down! Apostles deal with ruling spirits and they dispossess demonic ranks and governments. They are an office of mature believers who God specifically calls to that office.

Ambassadors and the Ministry of Reconciliation

"Now then we are ambassadors for Christ, as though God did beseech you by us: we pray you in Christ's stead, be ye reconciled to God" (2 Corinthians 5:20). First of all, Paul wasn't talking about everyone in this passage of scripture. When he said "we", in context, he was referring to himself and the apostolic team that accompanied him. Ambassador in the Greek is the word "presbeuo" (pres-byoo-o) and stems from the Greek word for elder, "Presbeuo"; this word stems from the word "presbuteros" (pres-boo-ter-os) which is defined as: elder, referred to those who were older in age, advanced in life, a forefather, and those who in separate cities managed public affairs and administered justice (ekklesia).

Apostles are mature men and women of God who are entrusted with ambassadorial authority and power. This is why true apostles cannot be babes nor can they work with babes. Babes in Christ cannot handle the weight and responsibility of government; God never trusts a baby with government. Anyone who enters into any office for the first time will be a babe in that office, but they will not be a babe in their Christian walk. You can have the power of an office before you fully operate in the authority and governmental function of that office. Because of this, many people are fooled into thinking that they are more advanced spiritually then they really are.

To be an ambassador of the United States you must meet certain educational, work, communication, and leadership qualifications. There is no difference in the kingdom! We must have mature qualities for a mature office. Apostles are called by God, but they must be trained in their understanding of how to execute the functionality of their office. This takes time and processing. There are too many people who are calling themselves apostles, but don't even meet the basic qualifications of the office. God doesn't even deal with them on a governmental level! Listen, if all God deals with you about is "church stuff" then I can guarantee that you're not called to be an apostle.

The Father has special dealings with His special messengers. Also, speaking of special, one of the meanings of the word apostolos is special messenger. If there is nothing special about your message then you are not an apostle. If the depth of your word can be compared to everyone else then you are not an apostle. I'm not trying to be critical, but as a fellow apostle, father, and brother in the faith, I have been assigned the task in this chapter to reveal the ancient basic function of the apostleship. Sadly, many who carry the title don't even do half of what I am describing and don't even understand the true purpose and function of this office.

Apostles call God's people to be reconciled with Him and were first to be given the ministry of reconciliation. Reconcile in the Greek is the word “katallasso” (kat-al-las-so) and it means: to change, exchange as coins for others of equivalent value, and return to favor with. Katallasso is made up of two Greek root words; the first one is “kat” (kat-ah) which means "down from" and is defined as: coming down from a higher to a lower plane with a special reference to an end point and relates to humbling oneself. A true apostle will confront your pride, bring you down from your lofty place, and cause you to come to the end of yourself.

The second word is “allasso” (al-las-so) which means to change or transform. Being reconciled to God has everything to do with humbling yourself so that transformation can take place. In this place, you will find yourself maturing and functioning according to God's original intent for His people. Apostles are charged with bringing humility to a people or region so that transformation can take place; without humility there is no change. This is executed through preaching and the demonstration of the kingdom by God's delegated authority and power invested in the office for the advancement of His empire. Apostles demand change and conformity to the kingdom of God because the kingdom required it first.

This is why the personality of the apostle can be very commanding at times. They may even seem insensitive or overbearing, but you must understand that apostles are generals, ambassadors, and are set aside by God for war, conquest, and culturing. These things are ingrained into their personality and to walk with them you must be able to be handle strict authority and command. They are not controlling! If they were, then you must also consider military drill sergeants or generals controlling every time they give a direct command. Only babes in Christ scream and holler about control!

When you are around authentic apostles, you feel the pressure to change. You will feel the pressure to relinquish all of your “bright ideas” and "what you think you know" to embrace the doctrine of that apostle. Now, to the carnal immature Christian this may sound very cult like or controlling. Even though cults are typically associated with this method, it does not mean that the original model of leadership was not sanctioned by God. Your hurt and bitterness does not change God's law. The scriptures tell us that the early Church continued steadfast in the apostles’ doctrine (Acts 2:42). The apostles received their doctrine from Jesus Himself. Paul also said that no one taught him the gospel, but He received it by revelation of Jesus Christ (Galatians 1:11,12).

Apostolic revelation becomes apostolic doctrine to the Church; the Apostle's doctrine was the revelation of Jesus given directly to them and taught to the Church. Apostles are called to change and conform you to what they have received from the Lord; this is why apostles must have continual direct fellowship with the risen Lord Jesus Christ. You cannot be an apostle and not have a face to face relationship with Him. How can you be an ambassador for a kingdom or king you never met face to face? How can you represent the King and His kingdom if you don’t know the King? You cannot effectively or accurately represent someone that you don’t know by face.

The Sunagoge and the Oikos

Apostles are the ambassadors and generals of the kingdom of God. They lead the mission in causing the enemy to lose ground in regions, territories, and in the lives of people; they cause the enemy to lose ground, his place of authority, and then they establish Godly spiritual government in that area. One of the major purposes of apostleship is the establishment of the Ekklesia. The Ekklesia is different from the regular congregation or household of faith model that we are accustomed to. “Oikos” is the Greek word for family or house. For example, if I was to say that I am head of the Blair household, that would be considered an oikos. Another Greek word that I would like to examine is “sunagoge”. This is where the word "synagogue" comes from and it is defined as: a congregation or a coming together of households to make an even larger household.

During that time in order to be considered a sunagoge, at least ten houses (oikos) had to come together and is similar to what we do today. A local church or congregation can be made up of many families coming together. Most believers today are apart of the sunagoge (household of faith). Most believers are not apart of the Ekklesia. There's a huge difference between the two. You must be committed to maturity to become a son of God and be an official part of His ekklesia. This has nothing to do with how long you been going to church or how old you are. You can be old and still foolish! This has everything to do with allowing God to get to the root of who you are in your fallen state so that true Christ likeness can be developed in you.

Diversity of the Ekklesia

We have limited the apostolic function to local congregations only. This is frustrating to the apostolic mantle and purpose. The Apostle's main function is the establishment of the Ekklesia, which does not have any religious meaning whatsoever; it’s a governmental word. I’m not just talking about “church” government, this is kingdom government that God is establishing to govern whole spiritual geographies. An example of this is the Jerusalem counsel. People tend to think of apostles as religious leaders. We have limited the apostolic to the affairs of a religious institution. When Jesus said the gates of hell would not prevail against His ekklesia, He was saying that the gates of hell will not prevail against His government and the officers of His government.

This scripture does not apply to everybody. Only the Ekklesia has the authority to deal with the gates of hell in a region or territory, not the oikos or sunagoge. It's the job of the Ekklesia to close those demonic portals in their assigned region and it is called to rule and protect their spiritual geography. They are also called to reinstitute the rule of God in the earth by dispossessing demonic rank and dethroning them over our assigned regions, territories, state, nation, etc. The kingdom is spiritual in origin; however it's effect will impact the kingdoms and nations of this world.

The senate of Rome and the original twelve apostles were called the Ekklesia. The Jerusalem counsel was also an ekklesia model of government. The Sanhedrin was made up of seventy elders and were called the Ekklesia consisting of the high priest, chief priests, and other elders; the elders were popular or proven businessmen and civic leaders. The kings court, princes of the land, and religious leaders also made up the Ekklesia of Israel. This explains why the apostles should be versatile in their natural and spiritual affairs. Those who have a true apostolic mantle will be able to raise up all kinds of people, especially those who have kingdom dealings or assignments in secular areas. People that say they are apostles, but are limited to raising up "church folks" to do "church things" are not real apostles.

Even if a particular apostle isn't called to go into a certain sector of secular society, he or she will still have the grace to equip that person for their assignment. Since apostles understand the kingdom and have received wisdom from God, they are able to give instruction concerning a person's assignment. A council full of "church folks" will always see or advise through the lenses of organized religion. The Ekklesia should be diverse and consist of people who have a kingdom understanding or perspective of the world around us. They are not people with their head in the sand waiting on Jesus to come back to rescue us out what we are supposed to fix. Half of our job as the Ekklesia is overthrowing and replacing demonic government. “When the righteous are in authority, the people rejoice: but when the wicked beareth rule, the people mourn” (Proverbs 29:2). We need righteous people in authority! The ekklesia model is a guaranteed way for the righteous to get into a place of authority. The righteous being in authority is not just about being in places of influence in society, it’s also about a great quantity of righteous mature people coming into a place of influence. Authority in this passage of scripture is the Hebrew word “rabah” which means: to become great, to become many, or to become numerous.

The problem is not the fact that there isn’t ANY righteous people in authority, we just don’t have ENOUGH righteous people in authority. This is why there is still mourning in the land. We need the Ekklesia to establish righteous rule in places of influence. This will only happen if people are raised up with an accurate understanding of the kingdom of God and they’re sent to these places. Not only that, but to also have the spiritual authority to advance the kingdom in that sector or place of influence. This is a strategic way to conquer territory and advance the kingdom. Do you now see why it is so important for the people of God to mature?

Apostolic Warfare

The weapons of our warfare are not carnal. We’re not fighting against people, but against strongholds. “For though we walk in the flesh, we do not war after the flesh: For the weapons of our warfare are not carnal, but mighty through God to the pulling down of strong holds; Casting down imaginations, and every high thing that exalteth itself against the knowledge of God, and bringing into captivity every thought to the obedience of Christ" (2 Corinthians 10:3-5).

An apostle's fight is against imaginations that have become strongholds in the lives of the people; we combat what dominates the thought life in our jurisdiction and are anointed to demolish these strongholds that are contrary to what God is doing or revealing. Strongholds keep people in bondage which prevents them from maturing. In this scripture, Paul is defending his apostleship at the Church of Corinth; they accused him and his team of being carnal. Paul had to remind them of who he was as an apostle and of his jurisdictional realm of authority that included them.

Carnal minds will see spiritual things from a carnal perspective and is always offended by kingdom authority and structure; it is always offended by authority that's outside of their jurisdiction. Apostles cannot operate from religious authority in order to cast down these imaginations. We have to demonstrate kingdom authority and power to eliminate strongholds in a region or territory. We have to culturize the people by casting down their vain imaginations through the process of destroying demonic governmental structures. If you want to know the principality of a region, discern the mindset of the majority of the population; principalities establish strongholds by ruling their imaginations.

The goal of the apostolic is to change culture by first changing mindsets. Apostles are cultural transformers; they stood in the counsel of God, received His blueprints and instructions, established a team (the Ekklesia) to help execute the instructions, and are able to replicate what they have received from the Father. Apostles are called to make the earth look like heaven. How do they do it? They lead the mission in the extraction of the enemy's ground by advancing into the territories as a general, establish kingdom culture, and rule as governor of those regions. This is why apostles are always militant because they're looking to gain ground for the kingdom of God. They have received strict orders and have been mandated to carry them out. Once the ground is conquered, the apostles with the Ekklesia, can rule from a place of rest. You may not agree, but religious thought patterns will create strongholds in your mind. This concept is very ancient and was believed and carried out in biblical times. The twenty-first century church is so behind! We cannot limit the apostleship to what we consider to be the Church. It existed before the Church! It's the apostleship that has the grace from God to help transition the Church into becoming governmental.

We must understand the apostleship and discern true apostolic voices in the body of Christ. We must hear and take heed to what these apostles have received directly from the Throne. There is a level of maturity that can only be reached when we submit to the doctrine and chiseling of a genuine apostolic governor, general, and father. Part of our process of maturity is submitting to this chiseling and governance. It's time for us to come into the full measure of maturity that can only come from the apostolic dimension! True apostles of the twenty-first century will not only mature the Church, but also will realign her with God's original intent for man.

Chapter 5

Rank and Status in the Kingdom

"And God said, Let us make man in our image, after our likeness: and let them have dominion over the fish of the sea, and over the fowl of the air, and over the cattle, and over all the earth, and over every creeping thing that creepeth upon the earth" (Genesis 1:26).

It was God's original intent for us to be a mature ruling class of people on earth with all power and dominion over everything that He made. We are the Ekklesia and it's in our DNA to rule; we have the highest rank on earth by heaven's standard. Because of the fall of Adam, we have inherited defeat and subjugation instead of dominion. This is what causes major conflict within ourselves. We have two seeds in us fighting one another for dominance. Originally, we were designed to have and exercise dominion. This is why going through an authentic process is so important! God will address all of our fallen qualities that were inherited from the fall of Adam and Eve, and are designed to prevent us from exercising ultimate dominion righteously.

The prerequisite for having dominion in the earth for the kingdom of God is being conformed to the image and likeness of God. If we do not understand this, then we will not be able to accomplish much in the kingdom of God. Image is the external representation of God. It is what people see when they look at you and is externally demonstrated in how you represent Him. Likeness is the quality of being like God in character. If we as believers do not master these attributes, then we will never enter into our royal identity as mature sons of God. The Church has adopted a pauper and defeated mentality that has shaped our minds into believing according to a system that causes us to fall short. It is because of the fall of Adam and Eve that we have inherited a lesser nature than what we were predetermined to inherit. This is why when we submit to a true process in the Lord, all of our fallen attributes are exposed, addressed, and evicted.

Lets look at the word “said” in this verse. The Hebrew word is “amar” which means: to command, to promise, to intend, and to be told. So when God said "let us make man in our image and after our likeness, and let them have dominion," He was giving a command for us to execute His original intent for us. We are to do on earth what God does in heaven. Glory to God! On earth, man was supposed to be who and what God is in heaven. This is His original design and mandate for us along with being commanded to have dominion. Dominion is a MANDATE from God and is defined as: an official order, decree, or commission to do something. Sounds very much like the kingdom to me!

Not only that... it is authorization, approval, and endorsement to carry out what one has been ordered to do. In the beginning, God commanded that man have dominion. It was this commissioning from God that gave us authority and heavenly sanction to carry out the duties of having dominion over everything God made. But in order to have dominion you must first be in His image and after His likeness. God will not expect us to carry out a command without giving us all that is needed to execute it. He is not that cruel or
unfair. We must learn what we have and what has been made available to us.

The Image of God

Let's deal with the word "image" for a moment. Image is the external representation of God. We are not just called to have Godly character, but also called to have a Godly image. Character is extremely important; however, we are also called to demonstrate God and His kingdom openly in the earth. It is not just about character, it is also about an external demonstration. I'm a strong advocate for having character and most of this book is about developing the character of Christ in you through processing. I find it interesting that image is mentioned first before likeness. This means that God cares about looks and image just as much as He cares about who we are in our character. This also tells us that what you do determines who you become. For example, “as a man thinketh in his heart, so is he” (Proverbs 23:7 KJV). You cannot demonstrate what you do not believe is possible. Why is this? It’s because the mind controls every facet of your body and is scientifically proven.

When you change your mind, you change your functionality. Matthew 12:34 tells says, “out of the abundance of the heart the mouth speaks.” (KJV). Whatever your heart is full of will be revealed in your speech and when your thinking changes, so does your conduct and speech. This is how believers truly experience transformation. "...but be ye transformed by the renewing of your mind..." (Romans 12:2 KJV). Transformation is not just inward, but it is also outward. Your state of mind dictates your state of life and how you function. When you continually do something on a consistent basis, it begins to shape your habits and priorities. It starts in the heart, but the manifestation of what God has commanded us to do will been seen through regular application of what is rooted in our heart. This is why we must allow God to reshape our thought process. In order to be like God you must think like God. Mind renewal causes transformation which will in turn cause major changes in our conduct and character.

This is why it is important to do the same thing that the Lord told Joshua to do. "This book of the law shall not depart out of thy mouth; but thou shalt meditate therein day and night, that thou mayest observe to do according to all that is written therein: for then thou shalt make thy way prosperous, and then thou shalt have good success" (Joshua 1:8).

This passage of scripture deals with speech and thought. When they are in alignment with God, prosperity and success becomes our portion. When we begin to think and talk like God, then we can function like God as He commanded us from the beginning. Adam already had a belief system built into him through the relationship that he had with God. He taught Adam face to face everyday when He visited him in the cool of the day (in the morning). Biblical meditation is to fill your mind with the word of God and to repeat repetitiously what you are filling your mind with. It is to constantly speak in alignment and think upon things of kingdom origin. Many wizards and witches today are very successful at what they do. They prosper because they meditate on what they believe and they discipline their lives according to what their mind is set on; many of them are successful at creating and releasing evil from the spirit world into the natural world.

When you believe, think, and speak things that align with the kingdom of God then you have no choice but to produce kingdom results. So yes, God does care about how we present Him and ourselves in His name. Jehovah is a God of presentation and demonstration. He likes to throw His weight around and we're called to throw His weight around too! Being in His image deals with how we represent God through presentation and external actions. It reveals who we are, who God is, and who we are in Him. We're called to display love, mercy, glory, signs, wonders, wealth, dominion, power, authority, etc. and this will only happen when we think and speak in alignment. "If ye then be risen with Christ, seek those things which are above, where Christ sitteth on the right hand of God. Set your affection on things above, not on things on the earth" (Colossians 3:1-2).

"Finally, brethren, whatsoever things are true, whatsoever things are honest, whatsoever things are just, whatsoever things are pure, whatsoever things are lovely, whatsoever things are of good report; if there be any virtue, and if there be any praise, think on these things. Those things, which ye have both learned, and received, and heard, and seen in me, do: and the God of peace shall be with you" (Philippians 4:8-9).

We are urged as believers to set our minds on heavenly or kingdom things and to do what we meditate and set our minds on. This speaks of being in total alignment with the character of God and the agenda of heaven and takes daily discipline and complete death to self. This is also how you reform your character to Christ's. What you decide in your heart to do and become will shape how you live. This lifestyle change will invite God to do a supernatural work in your soul and spirit. The reason is because when one seeks to align himself with God and His purpose for their existence, it will cause an incredible hunger to be birthed in you.

"Draw nigh to God, and he will draw nigh to you. Cleanse your hands, ye sinners; and purify your hearts, ye double minded" (James 4:8). We are commanded to draw near to God and in our drawing near process we are also commanded to cleanse our hands and purify our hearts. This happens in our initial action towards aligning our lives with His purpose for our existence. The closer you draw near to God in relationship the more exposed you will become. This exposure is not for the purpose of condemnation, but to cause us to deal with those things inwardly that make us less like Christ and less than who we were called to be. You cannot skip this process! Every encounter should change you to be more like Him. The closer you draw to God the more your character will become refined; it is the process of transformation. The reason for is because we are born and shaped in iniquity from our conception to our birth; this goes beyond falling into a particular sin. This has to do with the nature of who we are inside and out. You cannot cast out our nature, it must be processed out. When we draw near to God the dirtiness of our heart is revealed and we begin to see our double-mindedness. His holiness points out our imperfections and He highlights the things that will keep us from inheriting our birthright. When drawing near to God, you must be prepared for your heart to begin a process of cleansing and for your mind to go from being unstable to single-mindedness.

The Likeness Of God

Likeness is the quality of having God's character. This is what maintains your transformation and keeps you pure. When you are conforming to God's image, you are being trained to do what God does. When you're conforming to God's likeness, you are being trained to have His character. Together, they maintain a balance in us and eliminate any potential for an extreme abuse of authority and power; you also learn love, mercy, true faith towards God, judgements, and so much more. After you've been trained to function like God, which results a change in your thought process and character, you are also trained to be different because you think differently. When you truly believe in who you are supposed to be, then you begin to talk and live like it by conforming your life to it. It changes the way you view, interact, and address people.

A change in belief will result in a change of character. When you're in God's likeness, you possess the fruit of the spirit, as stated in Galatians 5:22-23, and you will have a hunger and thirst for dominion and rulership. You must possess the inward fruit and character of God in order to see this in your life. You cannot fully do what God does if you do not allow yourself to be conformed to His character; you must have His character to rule like Him and you must learn to love like God in order to be like God. This is also why man was made "after" His likeness. Why after?

The reason is because it is something that we must pursue. We must pursue the character of God to be formed in us... This is what the process is all about! Power with no character can destroy the world. Great power from God is only given to very few people. We must allow the character of the Father to be developed in us by submitting to His methods of character development.

Refuting A Pauper Mentality Among Believers

In order for us to come into the fullness of our God given identity, we must get rid of the pauper mentality. A pauper is defined as a very poor person; in the Hebrew culture, a pauper would be defined as a slave. Slaves have no inheritance and the only legacy they leave is to pass slavery to the next generation. A pauper is raised to be insignificant and is accustomed to being valued less than the rest. They have a poor self portrait of themselves, speak lowly, and carry themselves as being on a low grade; a pauper is trained to be insignificant. When you think like a slave you can't properly rule as a prince or king. In the years to come, God will begin to bring the hammer down on this type of mentality in the body of Christ. This mentality is immature!

As long as you are immature you are no different from a servant, but when you are mature you are given a government, as stated in Galatians 4:1-2. The Lord showed me that this is why Moses was raised in Pharaoh's house. If he was born as a slave his mind would have been conditioned to be a slave and he couldn't have embraced the mandate of a deliverer to free God's people from slavery. It would have taken him longer to prepare for God to raise him up as a deliverer.

A slave cannot deliver a slave from being a slave; only a free man can teach other people how to become free. Pharaoh's house shaped Moses' mentality to being a prince which made it easier for God to position and mantle him with kingly dominion. He was accustomed to being honored as royalty. Even though he chose to suffer with the Hebrews instead of living in Pharaoh's house, his authority and mentality was royal and as a ruler. The time spent in Pharaoh's house shaped his mind to receive the kingdom of God and for rulership.

It was easy for Moses to perform powerful and authoritative arrays of the kingdom because he was trained in royalty. It's easier for those who understand royal principles to access the power of the kingdom. A pauper mentality must be challenged among the community of believers in order for us to be effective in demonstrating the fullness of the kingdom in our generation. We must allow God to challenge all of our inferiority complexes to bring us to a place of royal standing with Him. When you submit to a true process in God, a pauper mentality will be challenged in your life!

Understanding Authority And Rank

"And when Jesus was entered into Capernaum, there came unto him a centurion, beseeching him, And saying, Lord, my servant lieth at home sick of the palsy, grievously tormented. And Jesus saith unto him, I will come and heal him. The centurion answered and said, Lord, I am not worthy that thou shouldest come under my roof: but speak the word only, and my servant shall be healed. For I am a man under authority, having soldiers under me: and I say to this man, Go, and he goeth; and to another, Come, and he cometh; and to my servant, Do this, and he doeth it. When Jesus heard it, he marvelled, and said to them that followed, Verily I say unto you, I have not found so great faith, no, not in Israel. And I say unto you, That many shall come from the east and west, and shall sit down with Abraham, and Isaac, and Jacob, in the kingdom of heaven. But the children of the kingdom shall be cast out into outer darkness: there shall be weeping and gnashing of teeth. And Jesus said unto the centurion, Go thy way; and as thou hast believed, so be it done unto thee. And his servant was healed in the same hour" (Matthew 8:5-13).

A centurion was usually a commander of at least eighty men. The first thing spoken of was the fact that he was under authority, before mentioning that he was in authority; if you're not under authority you have no legal right to be in authority. Understanding this is key to operating legally in the kingdom of God. The centurion was trained in military and governmental rank. He understood the operation of a kingdom's governmental structure. Because this man was trained in a kingdom structure, he was able to identify it and the kingly functionality of Jesus. Those who are trained in government can recognize government. Those who are trained in royalty can identify royalty and receive from royalty; however, those who are not under proper kingdom governmental authority are not in the kingdom. This is the problem with the Church today! We're so quick to defy authority when we don't agree with it.

You don't defy God's authority structure just because your flesh doesn't agree. This is sinful and wicked in the eyes of God. First of all, before we can understand our identity we must understand who our superior is. Every soldier is able to recognize their superior officer and every other superior that is over their superior officer. This is kingdom! The process helps you to recognize and understand the kingdom of God and how it functions. When you understand the upward chain of command and honor it properly, you have the spiritual backing of every superior over you when giving commands to those under you. Being properly aligned with authority gives you all of heaven's backing when speaking within your measure or sphere of jurisdictional authority. This centurion understood who he was, the measure of authority he operated in, and that

Jesus' governmental measure was greater than his. This is why he called Jesus "Lord." He also understood that Jesus' measure of authority superseded Caesar's authority. Jesus operated from a government that ruled every other government, including Rome. If only believers could grasp this! We can save and change nations within one generation.

The centurion saw that Jesus operated from a greater government, consequently calling Jesus “Lord”. He also saw how Jesus and the twelve operated; they weren’t walking around like they were best friends, even though I believe a special bond developed among them. They were a family with a governmental structure and rank. I know we despise the word government and rank in our generation, but you will never fully understand the kingdom of God properly unless you receive this. The centurion recognized how structured they were and the supernatural support behind that structure. By knowing how to honor governmental authority, he drew from it and saw results. Many of us love to pull on God, but we refuse to completely submit to Him and His governmental structure. This is what many charismatics are missing. All we know is gold dust, angel feathers, tongues, holy laughter, and prophecy, but lack the authority to dethrone chief prince demons over our cities and dispossess demonic ranks. This is because though many of us preach the kingdom, we do not understand it like we say we do. If we understood it properly, then we would govern ourselves a lot differently before God and among one another.

We must realize that we were made to function in a kingdom like structure. We have been deceived into thinking that democracy is freedom... Free to choose our own leaders, free to make our own laws, free to live our lives anyway we want, free to indulge in all that our flesh desires. This is freedom perverted! In reality, it’s flesh on display and shows how completely resistant and carnal we really are. Democracy is government by the people, exercised either directly or through elected representatives. This is not the way God has structured His kingdom! Notice in the scriptures how God raises up one man as the set gift and officer to lead the people. Though that man may have officials in whom he has delegated authority, he still has the highest authority and power under God. God never creates people to then place a man over them... that's democracy! He creates a leader first, then he multiplies. That is God's perfect model of leadership. I will talk more about this later.

Imperial Authority

Understanding authority, your placement under and in it, is crucial to knowing who you are in God. Adam, through his imperial loins was supposed to birth kings and princes to occupy and rule the earth. An emperor is a king of kings; they birth and rule kings and are fathers to kings. We can see all throughout scripture where the imperial mantle was given to individuals to execute. For example, Adam, Noah, Abraham, Moses, Samuel, David, Solomon, Elijah, Jesus, Peter, and Paul, just to name a few. If you study their functions or ministries, all these men had an imperial mantle and mandate from God to produce kings out of their spiritual loins. Anything imperial speaks of being a king or having oversight authority over kings.

These men also had a role in birthing, fathering, ordaining, and setting other kings in place naturally or spiritually. Only emperors or those with an imperial mantle can give placement and identity to kings. Everyone does not have that authority. God gave these men something that no one else had in their generation. These men had the highest authority in the earth and in their generation. Hear me in the spirit! Anything imperial has to do with emperors. An emperor is a king of kings and gives birth to and governs kings. You must understand this! These men I mentioned above had the mandate of birthing kings or those with a kingly anointing and function in the earth.

They may not have been called emperors, but they had the rank and mantle of one. They were the top people of their day. God always has top men or women that has imperial authority to initiate the genesis of what heaven has decreed for the current generation. We must understand this in order to fully mature.

This is where the apostolic comes in. Apostles should possess a kingly anointing. Not what we see today from those who merely wear a title behind their name. Revelation of the kingdom and kingship was given to the apostles of the new testament. I believe that when the Lord gives you a revelation of a thing, He imparts the ability to function in it as well. I'm talking about the ancient functionality and office of the apostle that the chiefs of old walked in. During the time of the new testament you could not call anyone "king" except Caesar (who was emperor), or risk being incriminated for treason. But if you examine the apostles function closely you will see an imperial or kingly function within their office.

This is why I tell people that an apostle is not a church gift or office only. The offices of apostle and prophet predate the Church. You cannot subject something to the Church that predates it. They are the foundation of the Church and existed before it, making them kingdom offices in origin. Without the presence and revelation of apostles and prophets there is no kingdom. One of the functions of these precious offices is to bring the people of God into their royal identity. I know that's a bold statement, but we must realize that the bible is a kingdom book. This book is mainly about a king, His kingdom, the children of His kingdom, and the king's dealings with His children. All of this was revealed by and given to apostles and prophets to steward and deliver. I'm not saying that the apostles and prophets are the "in all" and "be all" of the kingdom of God. What I'm saying is that they are the measuring stick. We cannot get around or ignore what God has invested in these offices for His body. Apostles and prophets are supposed to bridge any gap that exists between believers and the kingdom world. The apostolic and prophetic offices are supposed to serve as gateways into a new world - the kingdom world. No believer on earth can get around this! You cannot mature without these offices in your life... along with the other three. This is why Jesus trained the twelve in the kingdom first; their apostleship came out of the kingdom.

Whenever God wants to do something new or set the precedence for a particular generation, He will always initiate it through someone who has imperial authority. This person will most likely operate in the apostolic office. I'm not limiting imperial power to just the apostolic, but we must understand that everything starts with the apostle because of what the Father has invested in that office. The apostle is the gateway into imperial and kingly power. Let them who hears, also understand! God will always send someone with imperial rank and authority to raise the bar and set the standard for what He wants done or revealed in that generation. All of the men mentioned earlier did something that no one else in their generation did and very few had their access to God. I'm not saying that it wasn't available to all, but that they were the first ones in their generation to have it.

The revelation these men of God had was pioneering and revolutionary. They produced sons and daughters who would become kings and princes (rulers) after the blueprint or model given to the imperial apostle... as I like to call them. Similar to Jesus being a priest after the order of Melchizedek, the sons and daughters birthed in the spirit become rulers in the kingdom of God following the order, blueprint, or design given by the imperial authority for their generation. This is a patriarchal function of apostolic fathering that very few are allowed to function in. These men of God possess the keys of the kingdom for their generation. There are many different keys that a believer can have, but there are special keys that are only for God's chosen to execute the imperial function.

The kingdom of God was not available to the gentiles until Peter used the keys of the kingdom, given by Jesus, to open it up to them. Though it was prophesied, it was never accomplished to that degree in Peter's generation. He unlocked something new from the realm of the kingdom that ended up spreading all over the world. This is what emperors do. All of us play a very vital and important role in God's kingdom. God may use one man to initiate a move, but that one man must mobilize people to help assist and execute the mandate. He must also birth and mobilize a holy nation of people who will advance the kingdom agenda of the Father for their generation. You must learn to discern God's chosen man and recognize who God is using to be a pioneer in your generation. All apostles do not have to grace to pioneer on this level. This is why many miss the kingdom because they ignore or dishonor imperial authority. The following are some examples of this:

1. Noah - Ignoring his warning about the flood and mocking him.

2. Moses - Israel always complained about Moses. Korah's company was swallowed up in the earth when they rebelled against him. Miriam was cursed with leprosy when she and Aaron came up against Moses.

3. Samuel - Israel wanted a kingdom model after the nations of the world. The problem wasn't wanting an earthly king, it was that they rejected Jehovah's imperial kingship over them.

4. Jesus - He wept over Jerusalem because of the destruction that would come upon them for rejecting and killing the apostles and prophets. This happened in 70 A.D. with the destruction of the city and the temple in Jerusalem.

5. Peter - Ananias and Sapphira dropped dead at the feet of Peter because they attempted to deceive him concerning financial giving.

6. Paul - Paul spoke blindness over Bar-jesus, who was also called Elymas the sorcerer, because he tried to turn the deputy official away from what Paul was preaching (read Acts 13:6-12).

These few examples illustrate the consequences of when you defy imperial authority; severe judgment will come upon you. If we are going to truly be in the kingdom of God, then we must learn to not only recognize rank, but also the special rank that God may give to certain individuals. Only the process can develop this kind of heart in you. It takes maturity to honor correctly!

You Cannot Separate God From the Man

There's a greater judgement that comes on you when you defy the imperial authority of the kingdom. You must recognize and acknowledge who God is with. Everything that God does in the earth always starts with a man (or woman) and that person is who God is with. Again, I'm not saying that He's with no one else, but God is not with everyone like He is with that chosen person. You can't honor God without honoring His chosen man. When God does something major through man, especially one of imperial rank or even kingly rank, He never detaches their name from the work. What do I mean? The scriptures say He's the God of Abraham, Isaac, and Jacob (Exodus 3:6).

God told Joshua that as He was with Moses, He'll also be with him (Joshua 1:5). Scripture also says that Jesus would be a prophet like unto Moses (Deuteronomy 18:15 Acts 3:22 Acts 7:37). When Elijah was taken in the whirlwind and Elisha received the mantle, he came to the Jordan river and said, "Where is the God of Elijah?" Then he smote the water with the mantle and it split in half (2 Kings 2:14). Paul received a powerful revelation of the gospel of the kingdom and he called it "his gospel" (2 Timothy 2:8 Romans 2:16 Romans 16:25). Get the picture? You cannot separate God from the man.

This is the problem! People think they can serve God and ignore the chosen man. Paul said in 1 Corinthians 11:1, “Be ye followers of me, even as I also am of Christ.” You can’t skip over the man and follow Christ. Yes, we’re all under Christ and should have a personal relationship with Him, but the ways and mysteries of Christ are not revealed to everybody in the measure that it’s revealed to the one who He has invested greater authority. Follow me as I follow Christ... everyone doesn't know where Christ is going! The Lord doesn't reveal His special dealings to everyone. “He made known his ways unto Moses, his acts unto the children of Israel” (Psalm 103:7). The ways of God were not revealed to Israel. God does not reveal His secrets to everybody. He chooses a man who is faithful and obedient to reveal His secrets.

It was through Moses knowing the ways of God that he was able to demonstrate the acts of God to Israel. I'm not saying that no one else can know God except the chosen man, but knowing God and knowing the depth of His ways are two totally different things. He may choose to reveal certain things about Himself to you, but that doesn't mean that you know His depths and secrets. According to Numbers 12:7 Moses was faithful in all of God’s house. In the Complete Jewish Bible verse 7 says, “...He is the only one who is faithful in my entire household.” First of all when God chooses a man, He’s going to choose someone who is going to be faithful. He may not be perfect initially, but he will be faithful to God in a special way. Moses’ faithfulness to God qualified him to be appointed the imperial chosen man of his generation. Don’t mess with a man who’s faithful to God!

We can’t change God’s standards because we don’t agree or because we think too much power has been given to one man. As it is in heaven so it is on the earth; the same system of governance in heaven is the same system of governance in His kingdom among His people upon the earth. Proper processing conforms you to God's standards. Take note:

I'm not saying that apostles are the only ones that can walk in imperial authority. The apostle serves as a gateway to access that level of authority. If you are willing to pay the price, you can have this too! Our job as apostles and prophets, is to teach you about your royal identity. We cannot teach you how to become something that we have not obtained ourselves. This is why it must begin with the apostles and prophets, then spread to the rest of the body of Christ.

The Importance of Maturity And What It Produces

"And the Lord God formed man of the dust of the ground, and breathed into his nostrils the breath of life; and man became a living soul" (Genesis 2:7). We must understand that Adam was made from the dust of the ground, but he was formed and awakened in a glorified state. Adam had perfect genetics and there was no record of sin in his DNA. I want you also to notice that God did not make Adam a little boy or a baby, he made Adam a full grown man. He was made a mature son with the wisdom of God downloaded into his psyche. This was how he was able to name all of the animals. Only a son (mature believer) can take part in and give identity to what God creates or initiates. That is the level of trust the Father invests in those who are mature in Him. A baby cannot start and sustain a major move of God. This is why God is looking for people who are willing to be matured to demonstrate a higher dimension of glory. Adam was familiar with the glory and this is why he was blessed by God to have dominion in the earth. You cannot have dominion without the glory of God and you cannot operate in the fullness of glory unless you are willing to become mature through processing. When the true glory and presence of God becomes your habitat, your natural born again instincts begin to emerge. The prince, king, or emperor in you will begin to emerge.

We must understand that God is trying to raise us to a place of maturity so that He can give us responsibility in His kingdom. We have become satisfied with gifts and offices and have forgotten they are supposed to help us carry out our divine responsibility. Without responsibility you have no rank in God's kingdom; each rank or office carries a responsibility. There are many today who take on an office or title, but they don't carry the weight nor do they execute the responsibility of that office. Actually, it's not about the office itself, but it's what God has invested in the office and what it produces... that is most important. The five fold ministry is charged to mature us in measuring up to Christ's stature and for governmental responsibility in His kingdom. The five fold ministry of this generation has failed in the execution of this responsibility.

Many want the honor of an office, but refuse to accept the responsibility of that office. This is immaturity at its finest! I can see this paradigm being challenged and shifting in the near future. The Holy Spirit spoke to me and said, "a greater demand to mature will come upon many five fold officers who have ears to hear and a heart to obey." "But let every man prove his own work, and then shall he have rejoicing in himself alone, and not in another. For every man shall bear his own burden" (Galatians 6:4-5).

You have a divine responsibility and a role in the maintenance (preservation, keeping, continuance) of God's kingdom; however, it's only through the process of maturity in allowing God to develop you as a son that you will discover who you really are and your placement in His kingdom. Verse 4 says, "let every man prove his own work." The problem is... people don't want to be proven they just want to be positioned. This is one of the quickest ways to be ejected out of the kingdom of God. Every office and function in the kingdom of God must be proven. There is no other way to be proven by God but to go through the process!

You must be proven in order to be legitimized. You must be able to bear the burden of what you are being proven for. I hear many apostles and prophets complain about their process and opposition as a result of being who they are. There is no point in complaining about something that will never go away. There will always be opposition; complaining is a major sign of immaturity. This is another reason why the process is important. The process builds endurance in you so that you can be strong enough to bear the burdens. "And after six days Jesus taketh Peter, James, and John his brother, and bringeth them up into an high mountain apart, And was transfigured before them: and his face did shine as the sun, and his raiment was white as the light. And, behold, there appeared unto them Moses and Elias talking with him. Then answered Peter, and said unto Jesus, Lord, it is good for us to be here: if thou wilt, let us make here three tabernacles; one for thee, and one for Moses, and one for Elias. While he yet spake, behold, a bright cloud overshadowed them: and behold a voice out of the cloud, which said, This is my beloved Son, in whom I am well pleased; hear ye him" (Matthew 17:1-5).

One thing that we must understand when reading this is that Jesus was growing in His sonship with the Father. Whenever God initiates you in any office, you must grow up into the fullness of that office through processing and time. John the Baptist baptized Jesus in the Jordan River, the Holy Spirit descends upon Him in the shape of a dove, and the Father spoke out of the sky and said, "this is my beloved son in who I am well pleased." Jesus is then led by the spirit of God into the wilderness to be tempted by the devil. He goes in full of the Spirit, but comes out in the power of the spirit; being full of the Spirit is for you, but the power of the Spirit is for ministry to others.

Later, Jesus is transfigured. Transfigured, in Greek, is the word "metamorphoo" which means: to change into another form. I propose to you today that this relates to His genetics.

Jesus was changed into another form meaning that the form he previously had didn't exist anymore. When you go through the process and obey God in everything, you will get to a place where He will begin to change your form. This goes all the way down to the genetic makeup of who you are. It is possible to walk in such intense glory that it effects you on a cellular level. I will talk more about this later...."For the Son of man is come to seek and to save that which was lost" (Luke 19:10).

Notice that Jesus didn't use the word "those", instead He said "that"; He came to seek and save that which was lost. What was THAT? It was everything that Adam lost in the beginning, but this time, Jesus made it well under a better covenant. This is why Jesus is called the last or second Adam. He is the final Adam because Christ is the perfection and completion of what God wanted to do with the first Adam.

"Having made known unto us the mystery of his will, according to his good pleasure which he hath purposed in himself: That in the dispensation of the fulness of times he might gather together in one all things in Christ, both which are in heaven, and which are on earth; even in him" (Ephesians 1:9-10). Paradise was restored through Jesus. The same supernatural environment that Adam thrived in, is available to us. This was the mystery of His will that all things in heaven and earth will be gathered together in Christ Jesus. Heaven is no longer distant!

The supernatural reality of God is no longer distant! This is not just available to certain people anymore, it is available to those who are willing to pay the price of being processed to maturity and to live and walk in it. It is available to those who are willing to take off Adam (old man) and put on Christ (the second or final Adam). It's one thing to experience this, another thing to live in this, but it's something totally different to actually move in this. Just because you experience the glory doesn't mean that you live or move in it.

Before Jesus went into the wilderness to be tempted of the devil, He only experienced and lived in the Spirit. After He passed His test in the wilderness, He began to move in the Spirit. This is why He was able to demonstrate the supernatural reality of the kingdom. You must go beyond the realm of experience only to live in and also move in the glory of God. People seem to think that by experiencing God they are mature. Regular experiences of the presence of God doesn't mean that you're mature. Every believer is supposed to regularly experience the presence and glory of God, but there comes a time in your walk where you are able to supply it. Not just His gifts, not just the anointing, but His presence and glory... there's a difference.

When you become a son you become a prince with God. "And he said, Thy name shall be called no more Jacob, but Israel: for as a prince hast thou power with God and with men, and hast prevailed" (Genesis 32:28). Power, in Hebrew, is the word "sarah" (saw-raw) which means: to contend, persist, persevere. When you become a son, you're given divine ability or power to overcome. The princely anointing is a battlefield anointing that causes you to get great victory; military power comes with the princely anointing. In his time of trouble, Jacob held onto God to the point of wrestling with Him until his hip popped out of place. Leading up to this, Jacob was on the run from Esau, he served Laban seven years in order to marry his daughter (Rachel), but was tricked into marrying Leah (her sister).

He then had to serve Laban another seven years in order to marry the woman he was supposed to marry - Rachel. When he tricked Esau, he was tricked too and received a dose of his own medicine. I believe this was God's way of judging the iniquity in him so he could get to a place of brokenness in that area. In that place of brokenness, God can begin to remove the iniquity from you and make you into a mature son through proper processing. Jacob went through a process that caused him to be broken. Sometimes God allows trouble as a form of judgment to get us to a place of brokenness and repentance. This can also happen when we allow God to process us. Once we truly repent that's when transformation can take place within us; this is how you become a son (mature believer) of God. It was through this process that Jacob was qualified to walk in imperial authority, but he first had to overcome as a prince.

Sons Of God

There are three different levels of maturity that we can reach in God. Discipleship, servanthood, and sonship are paralleled with being a babe in Christ, child of God, and son of God. When it comes to sonship we have to look at God's firstborn for our best example. "For whom he did foreknow, he also did predestinate to be conformed to the image of his Son, that he might be the firstborn among many brethren" (Romans 8:29). This means that Jesus is not the only son of God. He was the firstborn among many brethren and if they're brethren to Him then that means they are also sons to God. This can also be seen in Genesis 6:1-4 which reads, "And it came to pass, when men began to multiply on the face of the earth, and daughters were born unto them, That the sons of God saw the daughters of men that they were fair; and they took them wives of all which they chose. And the Lord said, My spirit shall not always strive with man, for that he also is flesh: yet his days shall be an hundred and twenty years. There were giants in the earth in those days; and also after that, when the sons of God came in unto the daughters of men, and they bare children to them, the same became mighty men which were of old, men of renown."

Many sources say that these were angels who came down and laid with the women of that day. But according to Hebrews 1:5, God never called any angel a son. I'm thoroughly convinced that these were not angels; however, they were heavenly beings. We have to realize that all heavenly beings are not angels. There are Cherubs, Seraphim, Four Living Creatures, Archangels, Angels, etc... read Isaiah 6:1-7, Ezekiel 1:3-14, and Revelation 4:8-9. Clearly there are different classes of heavenly beings, with angels being one of them. There was a distinct class of heavenly beings called the sons of God and Jesus was the firstborn among them. As it is in heaven so it is on the earth. Look at the twenty-four elders... the bible doesn't call them angels, but they are heavenly beings too. There's a difference between angels, other heavenly beings, and those who were called sons of God. Sons of God embodied the original intent of the Father. But they, just like Adam, choose to be less than who they are and started laying with the daughters of men. They forfeited their post and birthright for the temporary pleasures of a fallen world. It is possible to lose your sonship status by continually following this example.

Becoming A Lesser Being

The concept of sonship was originated in heaven. The sons of God in Genesis 6 were not angels. They were heavenly beings who possessed the DNA of the Father, but allowed iniquity to be formed in them just like Lucifer. They no longer had perfect genetics, submitted themselves to a lower nature, and lowered the standard of God for their life. "And the angels which kept not their first estate, but left their own habitation, he hath reserved in everlasting chains under darkness unto the judgment of the great day" (Jude 1:6).

This has been translated as "angels", but let's look at this as a mistranslation and compare this to the sons of God as stated in Genesis 6. When you submit yourself to a lesser identity and a lower nature, you produce an abomination. The sons of God didn't keep their post. When they allowed seeds of a lesser nature to take root, it produced iniquity in them causing them to defy God, and to produce an abominable offspring. A similar thing happened with Lucifer as described in Isaiah

14:12-14 and Ezekiel 28:12-18. Lucifer allowed pride (a lesser nature) to pervert his purity and cause him to rebel against the Father. He ended up taking a third of the angels of his division with him (read Revelation 3:4).

This is a problem with man today. From Adam up until now, we have been subjected to a lesser nature, a lesser reality, a lesser way of living... a lesser everything! Adam's sin caused him to produce a race of lesser beings (fallen humanity) on the earth that was subject to the earth, sin, and corruption. In the beginning this was not so. All it takes is for one to become a lesser being and it will spread like wildfire! It started with Lucifer and spread to a third of his division; with Adam and Eve heeding the deception of the serpent, it spread to all of humanity. The good news is that what started with Jesus is also spreading to those who would mature into full sonship with the Father. Hallelujah!

The sons of God left their first "estate" according to Jude 1:6. Estate, in Greek, is the word "arche" (ar-khay) which is defined as: beginning or origin. They left their place of origin in God to chase the pleasures of a lesser life. The word "arche" originates from the word "archomai" (ar-khom-ahee) which means: to be the first to do anything, to begin, to be chief, leader, ruler. They were the first of their kind and the Father allowed them to possess authority in heaven to help Him rule. Remember... dominion is a mandate from the Father. They left their place of rulership and royal status, submitted to iniquity, and transgressed against God. When you embrace this lesser reality, you are more prone to sin against God. Jesus came to destroy sin so that the Father can restore His original intent in the earth through His sons. From the beginning, humanity has left their first estate in God, but Jesus came to restore it and it's through Him that we can obtain it.

The Status Of Being Chosen

"But ye are a chosen generation, a royal priesthood, an holy nation, a peculiar people; that ye should shew forth the praises of him who hath called you out of darkness into his marvellous light" (1 Peter 2:9). I've come to discover that though this is a familiar passage of scripture, many have neglected to study it properly to see what God is really saying. The word "chosen", in Greek, is the word "eklektos" (ek-lek-tos) which means: to pick out, the best of its kind or class, excellence, preeminence (the fact of surpassing all others, superiority), it is applied to a certain class of christians. According to the Greek language, this implied that God chose whom He judged fit to receive His favors, He separated from the rest of mankind to be peculiarly His own, and to be attended to continually by His gracious oversight. This was written to a certain class of believers who lived a life of holiness and suffered for their belief in Jesus. In order to qualify as being chosen of God, you must live a life totally set apart for the Father and you must be willing to be persecuted for your stance in His kingdom.

When you're chosen, you stand out from mainstream christianity. Many may not believe this, but there are certain ones who are mandated from the realm of eternity to stand out and suffer for His same sake. Because these people are mandated by the Father even from the beginning of time, they will end up with no choice but to do the will of the Father while the rest are given the option to. God knows who will choose Him and those who will refuse Him. Based on this knowledge

He uses all things according to His will to accomplish what He pleases. When you're chosen, you're the best of your kind, you've surpassed the rest of your brethren, and you've been given superior status in the kingdom because of your life of radical devotion and willingness to suffer for His name sake. When you're handpicked by the Father, it will show! Many are called, but few are chosen. There are some who can't escape God no matter how hard they try. They have a divine appointment with destiny. The chosen have a mandate on their lives and they have no choice but to serve God. On the other hand, there are also those who have the option to give their lives to God.

The King's Priest

The Complete Jewish Bible calls "royal priesthood", the King's cohanim (priest). Remember when God used Moses to deliver Israel out of Egypt, He told them that if they obeyed His voice and kept His covenant, then He was going to make them a kingdom of priests (read Exodus 19:5-6). This was God's intent for His people from the beginning, to make us priests with royal authority, rank, and backing. This is supposed to be the basic status for every believer, but because Israel didn't obey God's voice nor did they keep His covenant, God had to hand pick the tribe of Levi to serve in the tabernacle; and out of the sons of Levi, Aaron and his lineage would serve a priests. This change came after the golden calf incident in Exodus 32:26-29.

By not worshipping the golden calf, the Levites were blessed and chosen because their actions signified their loyalty to God. When the majority does not obey, God always has a remnant of people who will. There will always be people that are willing to pay the price to draw close to the Father and to deliver His people. When you don't feel the demand of God on your life, then you're not chosen for this. The priest represented the people before God, and they were charged to teach the people the laws of God. They bear the burden of the multitude and they have a love and passion for the Father, His holiness, and His righteousness to be established among the people.

When you're chosen by God you don't have the option to say no; you are marked for holiness and consecration unto the Lord. You are set aside from the rest of the people like the Levites (read Numbers 1:47-54). When you're faithful to God,

He marks you and chooses you to be set apart from the rest of the body. He gives you charge over His holy things and gives you a special status in the kingdom. Though every believer should have a priesthood and a special status with God, the truth is that many are not faithful enough to maintain such a relationship. It's not by works alone that you obtain a relationship with God, but your works are proof of your faith in Him and your devotion to Him. This priesthood is royal, it's not churchy! At this level in God you access things that transcends the church realm. This is a high honor and to obtain this you must love God with all of your entire being, pursue with all that you are, and be willing to suffer for His name sake. Do you love God and want Him that much to pursue Him on this level? It's something to think about! You must allow Him to address every area of your life and heart that keeps you from loving Him with your whole heart. This is what the process does; it prepares you to become His royal priesthood in the earth.

Chapter 6
Kingdom Genetics

"He that committeth sin is of the devil; for the devil sinneth from the beginning. For this purpose the Son of God was manifested, that he might destroy the works of the devil. Whosoever is born of God doth not commit sin; for his seed remaineth in him: and he cannot sin, because he is born of God. In this the children of God are manifest, and the children of the devil: whosoever doeth not righteousness is not of God, neither he that loveth not his brother" (1 John 3:8-10).

The word "born" is the word "gennao" in Greek, and is defined as: of men who fathered children, to engender (to bring into existence), and begat (formed through a process). It also comes from the root word "genos" which is defined as: kindred, offspring, family, stock, tribe, and nation; "gene" is associated with these words. Being born again has to do with your genetics. When you're born again, your genetics are changed to resemble Father Jehovah. When you truly become born again, something supernatural happens to you and the inherited power and nature of God becomes alive in you. When your genetics change, your nature changes too; if God is your Father then your genetics should prove that. Fathering is related to genetics.

As scientists began to decode the human DNA molecule, they found something quite unexpected—an exquisite "language" composed of three billion genetic letters. Dr. Stephen Meyer, director of the Center for Science and Culture at the Discovery Institute in Seattle, Washington said, "One of the most extraordinary discoveries of the twentieth century, was that DNA actually stores information—the detailed instructions for assembling proteins—in the form of a four-character digital code." (quoted by Lee Strobel, *The Case for a Creator*, 2004, p. 224). It is said that the amount of information in human DNA is roughly equivalent to 12 sets of The Encyclopedia Britannica – an incredible 384 volumes worth of detailed information that would fill 48 feet of library shelves! Dr. Stephen Meyer also said, "The coding regions of DNA have exactly the same relevant properties as a computer code or language."(quoted by Lee Strobel, The Case for a Creator, 2004, p. 237, emphasis in original)

Your DNA is like a miniature hard drive with the ability to store information concerning your life and the life of your ancestors. New research from the Emory University School of Medicine, in Atlanta, has shown that it is possible for some information to be inherited biologically through chemical changes that occur in DNA. This confirms that generational curses and iniquitous patterns can be passed generationally through our genetics. So imagine what happens when we become born again; we receive genetically all of the attributes of the Father. If God is truly your Father then you should have His DNA.

If Adam had it before the fall, then why can't we? Jesus (the second Adam) has restored what the first Adam lost, but with better promises. This is not just spiritual! Your natural genetics should resemble the One who birthed you into His eternal kingdom. Most of the Church today is not truly born again. As long as there's sin residue and generational curses embedded in your genetics, you will not fully become born again. I know this is a bold statement, but it's true! When you're born again the seed of God remains in you which makes it impossible to practice sinand for sin to reign in your life. Quite frankly, this is the work of Christ in our life!

"It is sown a natural body; it is raised a spiritual body. There is a natural body, and there is a spiritual body. And so it is written, The first man Adam was made a living soul; the last Adam was made a quickening spirit. Howbeit that was not first which is spiritual, but that which is natural; and afterward that which is spiritual. The first man is of the earth, earthy; the second man is the Lord from heaven. As is the earthy, such are they also that are earthy: and as is the heavenly, such are they also that are heavenly. And as we have borne the image of the earthy, we shall also bear the image of the heavenly" (1 Corinthians 15:44-49).

As I said before, if Jesus was the second or last Adam then Adam was the first Christ. When Jesus was on the cross, He was in the same state as Adam in his fallen nature. Even though Jesus became sinless, He was able to receive in Himself the record of Adam's fallen sin nature and died to it on the cross. "For he hath made him to be sin for us, who knew no sin; that we might be made the righteousness of God in him" (2 Corinthians 5:21). Jesus no longer possessed a fallen nature nor did He allow Himself to be subject to that fallen state. Through His victory and resurrection, we can also be delivered from our fallen nature. Hallelujah! This is truly what it means to live in the power of His resurrection.

1 Corinthians 15:45 says the last Adam became a quickening spirit. Quickening is the word "zoopoieo" (dzo-op-oy-eh-o) in Greek, which means: to produce alive and to begat (form through a process). Jesus was formed through a process by His Father for the purpose of becoming alive or born again. In His resurrected body, Jesus was a spirit being; He went back to the state that Adam was in, but being under a better covenant. He made the Father's original intent for us a tangible attainable reality. The natural body of Jesus became so glorified that it was received into heaven! Enoch and Elijah experienced the same thing. Genetically these men of God were so perfected, justified, and purified that they were able to

be received into heaven in their natural bodies. Glory to God! Imagine reaching such a place of glory and relationship with the Father that you can engage Him and all of heaven with your natural glorified spirit body. This is glorious! After the resurrection, Jesus was so glorified that He didn't want anyone to immediately touch Him. This is what true maturity in the kingdom is able to do for you. Just imagine being able to live in and demonstrate the realities of the kingdom world while living here on earth. In order to experience this, you have to be processed out of Adam and the base reality of this world to live in and from the kingdom world.

If we're to be conformed to His image like the scriptures say, then we too can become gloried in our bodies in a similar way. Part of our inheritance as believers is to be Christ in the earth. We can have glorified bodies while we're alive on the earth, full of light, power, and glory. When your DNA has been purged and only the seed of God remains, you're able to be transfigured, like Christ upon the mountain, so that the glory of the Lord can radiate through you and illuminate all darkness around you. When the light and glory of God is radiating and emanating from your DNA, darkness cannot live in you and cannot be around you without being exposed.

The key to seeing this in our lives is not just asking God to forgive our sin, but also asking Him to blot out and cleanse us from our iniquities. Forgiveness is instantaneous, but blotting out iniquities takes time and processing. Iniquity can be hidden, deeply rooted, or both. A time of exposure and processing is necessary for abstraction. If you truly want to be born again then you will have to go through this process and face what's in you and your family's bloodline that is still attached to you. For the record... not being actively involved in a particular sin doesn't mean that there's no record of it in you. We previously discussed that information can be passed genetically and some things come out later if they're not conquered early. If it's in your family line, then it's in you!

The Judgements Of The Lord

"Woe unto you, scribes and Pharisees, hypocrites! for ye pay tithe of mint and anise and cummin, and have omitted the weightier matters of the law, judgment, mercy, and faith: these ought ye to have done, and not to leave the other undone" (Matthew 23:23). "But woe unto you, Pharisees! for ye tithe mint and rue and all manner of herbs, and pass over judgment and the love of God: these ought ye to have done, and not to leave the other undone" (Luke 11:42).

Jesus rebuked the Pharisees for omitting the weightier matters of the law which were judgement, mercy, faith, and the love of God. When Jesus said "weightier matters", He meant that out of everything that is written in the scriptures, these are the most important. Among the weightier matters of the law are the judgements of God. Understanding judgement is one of the most important things to God. Judgement is the word "krisis" (kree-sis) in Greek, and it's defined as: a separating. Judgement also has other definitions in Greek, but this is the one I really want to point out. The judgements of God come to separate you and separate from you what God doesn't desire in your life. Anything contrary to the will of God will be judged when you submit to proper processing. Being one of the most important things to God, a weightier matter should also be one of the most important things to you.

Many times judgement makes us think about the wrath of God. We must understand that there is a difference between the judgement and wrath of God. The wrath of God will come if the judgements are ignored. This doesn't always happen, but it can and has happened. If we don't allow the judgements of the Lord to perfect us, then we will become bitter, stubborn, and reprobate before God. This will put us in a position of rebellion causing grace to no longer work in our lives (read Hebrews 10:29).

"The law of the Lord is perfect, converting the soul: the testimony of the Lord is sure, making wise the simple. The statutes of the Lord are right, rejoicing the heart: the commandment of the Lord is pure, enlightening the eyes. The fear of the Lord is clean, enduring for ever: the judgments of the Lord are true and righteous altogether. More to be desired are they than gold, yea, than much fine gold: sweeter also than honey and the honeycomb. Moreover by them is thy servant warned: and in keeping of them there is great reward. Who can understand his errors? cleanse thou me from secret faults. Keep back thy servant also from presumptuous sins; let them not have dominion over me: then shall I be upright, and I shall be innocent from the great transgression. Let the words of my mouth, and the meditation of my heart, be acceptable in thy sight, O Lord, my strength, and my redeemer" (Psalms 19:7-14).

God's law (instruction, direction, custom), testimony (witness evidence), statues (precepts-principles, rules, decree), fear (reverence, awe, deep respect), and judgements (justice - just behavior or treatment) all go hand in hand. We cannot have one without the other and think we're okay! They all deal with self governance according to the standard that God has set; judgement is included in this. We cannot truly be in right standing with God without facing His judgements in our lives. They are for our purifying and refining not our ultimate destruction. We must see this through the eyes of maturity and desire them more than riches.

Verse 11 says, "Moreover by them is thy servant warned." The judgements of the Lord can come in the form of a warning. He may address you personally, through a dream, a messenger, spiritual parent, or mentor. He addresses what He is separating from your life or from you. Remember, warnings are always futuristic. It comes to prevent you from acting on what's already in you and to deal with it at the root. It can also come to warn you by letting you know what's about to happen if you continue on the path that you're currently on. It comes to reveal what is in you that could hinder your destiny or shipwreck your ministry. Sometimes warning will even come in the form of trials to keep you from committing greater acts of sin later in life.

Verse 12 says, "Who can understand his errors? cleanse thou me from secret faults." It's hard for people to see their own errors. Many times our faults are secret and it takes for us to allow God's way of processing to expose what is hidden in us. "The heart is deceitful above all things, and desperately wicked: who can know it? I the Lord search the heart, I try the reins, even to give every man according to his ways, and according to the fruit of his doings" (Jeremiah 17:9-10). This scripture describes much of our maturation process. The heart is deceitful above all things. The first thing God sees in your heart is the deception that's keeping you from seeing your true self. The question is... "who can know it?" This was a rhetorical question. You can't know your own heart nor can you accurately identify what is hidden apart from God's processing.

Deceitfulness Of The Heart

Jeremiah 17:10 says that God searches your heart, then He tries it. The Father will identify and expose your hidden iniquity, and then He will try you in that area. You will go through the necessary processes to overcome and rid yourself of what has been exposed in you. Once your heart is tried by God, your reaction to His trial determines His action towards you. He gives every man according to his ways and the fruit of His doings. Many believers run from this and never mature; they resist the maturation process of the Father. Many become infatuated with gifts, offices, anointing, and supernatural manifestations, but they refuse to go to this depth with God. At the end of the day, all they have are gifts, offices, anointing, and supernatural manifestations; they never grow or advance beyond these things. They never really mature to a place where

God can entrust them with the full government and dominion of His kingdom. We must be willing to go on to perfection! We must allow the judgements of the Lord to expose our secret faults in order to mature into perfection.

God Resists the Proud

"Keep back thy servant also from presumptuous sins; let them not have dominion over me..." (Psalm 19:13). Presumptuous is the word "zed" in Hebrew, which means: to be arrogant and proud. The judgements of the Lord are designed to humble you and only proud people resist this process. The judgements of the Lord will keep you from sins rooted in pride. When you're prideful Leviathan is your lord, not Jesus. Job 41:34 says that Leviathan is king over all of those who are children of pride. According to James 4:6 God resists those who are proud and gives grace to the humble.

The more you humble yourself, the more you detach yourself from the lordship of Leviathan; you receive grace and divine enablement from God to overcome during your process. I will touch on this in more depth in a later chapter. This is key to understand when the Lord is processing you to maturity. How much pride you have in you will determine how intense God's dealings will be with you. Always remember that! Pride will always cause you to rebel against God, just like Lucifer.

Transgressions resulting from pride will not have dominion over you if you allow yourself to be submitted to the judgements of the Lord. When the law, statues, commandments, and fear of the Lord are not present in a person's life, the judgements of the Lord are not properly embraced. This is the work of grace in our life. God will judge our wickedness on earth so that we won't be judged for it when we physically die and stand before the Lord. That's love! After enduring the judgements of God, the words of your mouth and the meditation of your heart can be acceptable in the sight of the Lord (read Psalm 19:14). Your speech and your thinking will change. Just like David, you will come to know the Lord as your strength and your redeemer in your time of processing.

The Chastisement of the Lord

The judgements of God are also known as His chastisements or corrections. When God exercises judgement in your life, He's trying to change your character and the nature of who you are. You may endure wicked things from wicked people, but your focus should be on what God is trying to do in you. During this time, you will either become more purified or more wicked; you will become better or bitter.

"Wherefore seeing we also are compassed about with so great a cloud of witnesses, let us lay aside every weight, and the sin which doth so easily beset us, and let us run with patience the race that is set before us, Looking unto Jesus the author and finisher of our faith; who for the joy that was set before him endured the cross, despising the shame, and is set down at the right hand of the throne of God. For consider him that endured such contradiction of sinners against himself, lest ye be wearied and faint in your minds. Ye have not yet resisted unto blood, striving against sin. And ye have forgotten the exhortation which speaketh unto you as unto children, My son, despise not thou the chastening of the Lord, nor faint when thou art rebuked of him: For whom the Lord loveth he chasteneth, and scourgeth every son whom he receiveth. If ye endure chastening, God dealeth with you as with sons; for what son is he whom the father chasteneth not? But if ye be without chastisement, whereof all are partakers, then are ye bastards, and not sons. Furthermore we have had fathers of our flesh which corrected us, and we gave them reverence: shall we not much rather be in subjection unto the Father of spirits, and live? For they verily for a few days chastened us after their own pleasure; but he for our profit, that we might be partakers of his holiness" (Hebrews 12:1-10).

During the time of our chastisement, we must remove all sins and weights that would take our focus off of completing the race set before us. Our eyes need to be fixed on Jesus... He is our goal and prize! Our processing is to make us identical to Him. We must run with patience because this process will take some time; God wants to do a thorough and detailed work in us. We need to look to Christ's endurance as an example of how patient we should be in God's dealings with us. It's your faith that will see you through your process. I know this by personal experience! It's also vitally important to understand that faith works by love (read Galatians 5:6). Love and faith will help you through your process. Understanding God's love for you and your response to that love in faith is key. Another key is to love people unconditionally.

It pleased the Father to bruise Jesus (read Isaiah 53:10). So if it pleased Him to bruise Jesus, then it pleases Him to bruise (discipline) you and I. During this time, you will become bitter or you will become better. The judgements of the Lord will cleanse your faults and hidden iniquity. Our heart deceives us about ourselves all the time. We don't like to see the bad things about ourselves, but this is the path to true deliverance. "Confirming the souls of the disciples, and exhorting them to continue in the faith, and that we must through much tribulation enter into the kingdom of God" (Acts 14:22). Without tribulation to afflict the flesh, that thorn in your side to expose your pride, and the process, you will never enter into the kingdom of God.

"And lest I should be exalted above measure through the abundance of the revelations, there was given to me a thorn in the flesh, the messenger of Satan to buffet me, lest I should be exalted above measure" (2 Corinthians 12:7). You can see the judgements of the Lord at work in Paul's life to cause him to conquer pride. It is so easy for apostolic and prophetic leaders to become prideful because of the tremendous authority, power, and revelation that God invests in us. God allows certain things to happen, even the work of the enemy, to try those areas for exposure; tribulation is necessary. Our reaction will expose what's hidden in us. Affliction and tribulation can be a form of chastisement from the Lord. I'm not saying that all the affliction and tribulation we endure in life is chastisement from the Lord, but when it comes to God processing us to perfection, He will employ these things to humble us.

"He that committeth sin is of the devil; for the devil sinneth from the beginning. For this purpose the Son of God was manifested, that he might destroy the works of the devil. Whosoever is born of God doth not commit sin; for his seed remaineth in him: and he cannot sin, because he is born of God. In this the children of God are manifest, and the children of the devil: whosoever doeth not righteousness is not of God, neither he that loveth not his brother" (1 John 3:8-10).

The whole purpose of the chastisements or judgements of the Lord is to destroy sin and iniquity in your life. Isaiah 59:2 says, "But your iniquities have separated between you and your God, and your sins have hid his face from you, that he will not hear." Iniquity and sin cause a separation between us and God. Nothing can separate us from His love, but iniquity and sin can separate us from a continual deeper fellowship with Him. Jesus manifested to destroy this work in our lives, but we must understand that this kind of work is thorough and it requires time. Jesus died once and for all, but the reality of His death and resurrection must be worked out in us... this takes time. Many people think that salvation is automatic, but the scriptures tell us differently. Your salvation is not automatically obtained, but by the grace of God, it can be received through a process. The scriptures don't say we're automatically saved, it says we "shall be" saved (read Romans 10:13 and Acts 2:21).

"Shall be" is a progressive word which denotes that it's not automatic, but can be obtained if we remain in grace and allow the Lord's judgements to purify us. Remember, we're saved by grace through faith (read Ephesians 2:8) and it's through the working of grace in our lives that we receive this. The judgements of the Lord are God's work of grace in our life. "But he that shall endure unto the end, the same shall be saved" (Matthew 24:13). This is what the born again process looks like. Judgements remove anything that can or have the potential to separate us from God. 1 John 3:9 says that whoever is born of God does not sin. Until sin has no dominion over and in you, you're not born again.

This is how we identify the children of God and the children of the devil; they're identified by who has total governance in their life, not by inward fragmentations and divided loyalties between the kingdom of darkness and the kingdom of light. Jesus dealt with sin on the cross; however the judgements of the Lord address the sin nature in you. We teach people in church today that they become born again through a simple confession or through believing. Faith is the genesis of this process.

You have to be totally submitted to the Lord and His processes for your life to inherit this. It's not by your own personal works of self righteousness; it is accomplished by allowing the Lord to do His perfect work in you. The latter part of verse 9 tells us that we cannot sin because the seed of God remains as a result of being born again. For something to remain in you that means an abstraction is taking place. Once God is finished processing and removing hidden iniquity in you, nothing but God's seed will remain. This is why it's important to seek this! It's not enough to be like Jesus in certain areas. We should desire to be like Him in all things.

He's the perfect example and through submitting to the judgements and chastisements of the Lord, we can become perfectly aligned with His perfection. How glorious! This is the real meaning of submitting to His lordship and it's not impossible to accomplish. We as believers become comfortable with gifts, offices, and promotions in God, but that's not enough!

We should not desire His gifts and offices above His character being perfected in us. Those who don't submit to this process cannot become sons of God.

Citizens or Sons

What many don't realize is that you can become a citizen of the kingdom, but not be a son of the kingdom. There are different degrees of living in God's kingdom; your degree is according to your relationship status with the Father and whether or not you're willing to pay the price for intimacy. Just like in a natural kingdom, a son lives in the palace beyond the gates. When you're a son you are royalty. If you're not a son, then you are not allowed past the palace gates. We think just because we have had encounters with God that we have automatically arrived. This is deceptive thinking! Grace doesn't make you a son, but gives you the opportunity to become a son. You can be in the kingdom and not be a son. Let me explain before you totally dismiss what I'm saying. There's a difference between being a citizen of the kingdom and being a son of the kingdom. Sons have privileges that citizens don't. Sons have access to the king all the time while citizens only have access to the king at appointed times. You must understand the difference!

You must be born again to see and enter the kingdom. The DNA of the King and His kingdom must be the only thing that remains in you. Citizens are more concerned with civilian life; if you are concerned about how you're going to eat, live, survive, etc., then you are operating within the confines of civilian life in the kingdom. Sons will sacrifice these things (and more) for intimacy with God and knowing Him as Father. Sons don't worry about provisions because they have been tried in that area. Only sons can live in the palace... Hear me with your spirit! The carnal man won't understand this. Many believers don't know God as Father; they know Him as healer, provider, deliverer, and many other things, but only sons can know Him as Father. That is what will give you access to the greater depths of God. Many call Him Father, but they don't know Him as such. If you don't know Him as Father, then you won't understand what it is really like to be His son. Citizens are more concerned with their life in God, but sons seek to be like the Father in life. There is a difference! Citizens are more focused on the marketplace while sons indulge in the treasures of the palace. Marketplace ministry is needed, but eventually a son will outgrow it once they start living the "palace life" in the kingdom of God.

What is marketplace ministry? It's a form of evangelism or activity of believers that are targeted towards secular workplaces or other arenas of influence outside of the local church. This indeed has its place and is very needed! I believe that the kingdom of God should invade all sectors of society, but take a look at this for a moment... When you look at a natural kingdom, where is the market located? Surely it's not located beyond the palace gates! The marketplace is located in the heart of civilian life. Don't get me wrong, the market helps to fund the kingdom overall, but that is not proof of the kingdom's presence. Many believe and teach that it's the king that goes into the marketplace, but this is not true. You will never see a king leave his throne or palace to work the marketplace. If he truly needs or desires something from there, he will send other people for him.

Kings are beyond the market because they own the market! If you do not own the market, then you're not a king. When you're truly a son of God you possess the DNA of God; He is a ruler and a lord (owner). Much of what we call marketplace ministry is low level management that people mistake for ownership on a large scale. God is not a manager, He's an owner. He doesn't just own little stuff, He owns big stuff. We must understand the difference.

When you're truly born again, you're immersed and awakened to a whole new reality of God and His kingdom. In our DNA is the ability to have dominion, but we first must rid ourselves of all the other junk that attempts to suppress this part of us. Only the process can do that! We must get to the place where we are like Jesus before He went to the cross. "Hereafter I will not talk much with you: for the prince of this world cometh, and hath nothing in me" (John 14:3). This can only be done through submitting to the Lord's judgements and chastisements for our life so that we can become born again sons of God. The Father wants to make you greater than you are now so that you can live up to your full potential in the kingdom of God. This will only be accomplished through a greater level of submission to God's chastisements through processing for your life.

Chapter 7
Iniquity

In Hebrew, iniquity is defined as: something that is twisted or distorted. Anything that is not in alignment with God's perfection has an iniquitous nature. This is really important to understand. The origins of iniquity were discovered in the fall of Lucifer. "Thou wast perfect in thy ways from the day that thou wast created, till iniquity was found in thee" (Ezekiel 28:15). As long as iniquity is present within us, perfection will never be attained nor will it become a reality in our lives; it keeps us out of the realm of perfection in Christ. Scripture tells us that we are supposed to be conformed to the image of Jesus Christ who is our elder brother and perfect example (read Romans 8:29). Jesus became perfect like the Father and we are also commanded to become perfect, just like them (read Matthew 5:48).

There is an erroneous teaching in the church that says we cannot become perfect. This is so far from the truth and has no biblical support! This type of powerless teaching keeps many in the body of Christ in bondage. I'm not saying this to condemn those who are not perfect. What I am saying is that perfection is attainable in this life. The people of God need to be challenged to become perfect like their example, Jesus our Lord. What is the purpose of "trying" to be like Him if we are unable to be completely like Him? That doesn't make any sense! Jesus became perfect so that through His example we can become perfect too.

Our Call to Perfection

In Greek, perfect is the word "teleios" (tel-i-os) and it means: to be brought to an end, finished, wanting nothing necessary to completeness, and mature. Perfection has to do with maturity and embodying God's original intent for man before iniquity manifested. When you're perfect, you have become a finished product in God. This does not only apply when you die and go to heaven. When Jesus said to be perfect, He wasn't speaking about going to heaven. The Father wants us to be perfected while living on the earth. If we're to be conformed into the image of Christ and He became perfect, then we can obtain the same thing while living on earth. We need to stop making religious excuses as to why we fall short in this area in our walk with God! The word of God is clear on this subject.

God wants you complete and mature so that you can experience the full reality of His kingdom. Often I hear people religiously say, "though we will never be perfect, we should strive towards perfection." This is one of the most foolish, erroneous, and religious statements that I have ever heard! What's the point of striving towards something that you will never obtain? That's like getting married, having intercourse with your spouse in hope of being pleased, but never getting the pleasure you desire. What's the point of striving towards a pleasure that you will never behold? It sounds stupid doesn't it?! This is what false humility does to the church. It keeps us away from fulfilling the promises of God and embodying the totality of God's nature. False humility keeps you out of the realm of authority and dominion in Christ.

Iniquity is the main gate the enemy uses to gain entry into the lives of believers. It's the compelling force on the inside of you to do wrong, when you know it's wrong. It's what apostles, pastors, and other senior leaders don't conquer within themselves that passes down genetically to their children. Preacher's children are one of the main targets of the enemy regarding iniquity; many of them have the hardest time either serving God or overcoming sins while trying to serve God. Iniquity is the fall from perfection. Anything that does not reflect the image and likeness of God has an iniquitous nature and is twisted and perverted.

Iniquity, Sin, and Transgression

"Thou shalt not bow down thyself to them, nor serve them: for I the Lord thy God am a jealous God, visiting the iniquity of the fathers upon the children unto the third and fourth generation of them that hate me" (Exodus 20:5). God is speaking to His people in this scripture when He stated He is going to visit their iniquity, not their sin. Sin is the result of iniquity. Iniquity is the root that emerges all evil inside us. We have mastered confessing our sins, but we rarely deal with the depths of our nature that causes us to sin. We never really deal with our propensity towards sin or ask God to blot out our iniquities. We're constantly confessing our sins while committing the same sins we're confessing. If you have confessed your sin, sown seeds, prophesied, received prophecy, and believed God, and you are still overcome by misfortunes, then you don't have a sin problem... what you have is iniquity.

It's the iniquity that brings the curse. That is what God is coming after in you when you submit to a true process in the Lord. In the church, we are not taught to seek God for judgement of our iniquities. Many of us are too busy trying to cover them up instead of being brave enough to submit to God's process. Many refuse to face themselves which causes them to remain in bondage repeating the same cycles. As an experienced deliverance minister, I can cast out your demons all day long, but until you allow God to deal with your iniquities you will continue to go back to what you are seeking deliverance from. It's the iniquity that gives demons the legal right to remain or come back. I have seen this happen time and time again.

“And the Lord passed by before him, and proclaimed, The Lord, The Lord God, merciful and gracious, longsuffering, and abundant in goodness and truth, Keeping mercy for thousands, forgiving iniquity and transgression and sin, and that will by no means clear the guilty; visiting the iniquity of the fathers upon the children, and upon the children's children, unto the third and to the fourth generation” (Exodus 34:6,7).

Before I go any further I want you to note something. As I'm writing this, The Lord has instructed me to address this. We can clearly see that the mercy of God is required for forgiveness of iniquity. Without the mercy of God, you cannot be delivered from iniquity. Proverbs 16:6 says “By mercy and truth iniquity is purged: and by the fear of the Lord men depart from evil." Mercy comes before truth and in Greek, is the word “chesed” (kheh-sed); it is defined as: goodness, kindness, and faithfulness. Because of the Lord’s kindness and goodness towards us, we receive forgiveness and deliverance.

God’s goodness and kindness comes before His truth about our inner condition. One of the problems with the church today is we’re busy wanting to expose everyone's faults instead of being merciful and compassionate about where they are. God is not like that. Mercy doesn't condemn people for their condition. Mercy actually seeks to understand why they are in that condition in the first place. You must be merciful before addressing the truth about a person's condition. If God does this to us, then we should also do it to others.

The same measure of mercy you give will determine the measure of mercy you receive from God. “Do not judge, so that you would not be judged: for in which judgement you judge, you will be judged, and in the measure in which you measure, it will be measured to you" (Matthew 7:1,2 ONMB). This scripture is speaking about being judgmental, but is not talking about righteous judgement mentioned in John 7:24. There's a difference between judging righteously and be being judgmental. Righteous judgement is also accompanied by mercy.

Judgmental people are always critical of the shortcomings of others and are merciless when it comes to the fall of others; they would rather see judgement than mercy. "For he shall have judgment without mercy, that hath shewed no mercy; and mercy rejoiceth against judgment" (James 2:13). When you show no mercy yourself then you will have judgement without mercy; it triumphs over judgement. Hallelujah! If God who is all sovereign and all powerful is merciful then who are you or I not to be merciful? Surely we are no better than the Father.

In Exodus 34:6,7, we can see that iniquity, transgression, and sin are laid out. Many people believe that they are the same thing when they're not. Iniquity is the fallen and perverse inward nature of man. If you study the Hebrew word for transgression "pesha" (peh-shah), it's defined as rebellion. Transgression and trespasses are used synonymously in scripture and are called voluntary sin. Every time you do something you know is wrong you are committing a transgression.

Most trespassers see the sign that says "no trespassing" but they decide to ignore the sign anyway. The sign set the boundary for you not to cross. Trespassers rebelliously cross the lines that God has set in place. These people want what they want. They know what they are doing is wrong, but would rather deal with the consequences later and seek to avoid any consequences (if possible). "Sin" in Hebrew is literally defined as: missing the way, going wrong, or missing the mark. This is an involuntary offense against God. Though it is an offense against God, this is one out of pure ignorance. In my opinion, this is the rarest kind of offense (especially in the church) because when people sin, they consciously know that they are doing wrong most of the time.

"Surely he hath borne our griefs, and carried our sorrows: yet we did esteem him stricken, smitten of God, and afflicted. But he was wounded for our transgressions, he was bruised for our iniquities: the chastisement of our peace was upon him; and with his stripes we are healed" (Isaiah 53:4,5).

Transgression and iniquities are addressed here, but sin isn't. This is because unintentional sins are covered by the blood of Jesus and the grace of God. I'm not saying that they don't need to be confessed in order to be blotted out. What I am saying is that through the acknowledgement of confession of sin, your sin can be forgiven. There is no process to be free once sin is acknowledged and you repent of it. Sin will begin to disappear in your life as you mature in your relationship with the Lord. It's the iniquity and rebellion in you that must be processed out of your character, this is what God is after!

"Yet it pleased the Lord to bruise him; he hath put him to grief: when thou shalt make his soul an offering for sin, he shall see his seed, he shall prolong his days, and the pleasure of the Lord shall prosper in his hand. He shall see of the travail of his soul, and shall be satisfied: by his knowledge shall my righteous servant justify many; for he shall bear their iniquities" (Isaiah 53:10,11).

The cross of Jesus Christ addresses your iniquity. You can't receive from the resurrection if you don't embrace the fellowship of His suffering at the cross. If it pleased the Lord to bruise (discipline, chastise) Jesus then it will please the Lord to bruise you. This must be accepted in order to fully mature. In Hebrew, "bruised" means: to be crushed or broken. You have to be crushed and broken before iniquity can be removed. Iniquity makes you hard towards the will of God and must be broken through the process. Jesus justified many because He bore their iniquities. Until iniquity is removed there can be no real justification. The cross is a finished work, but that work has to be worked out in us. Philippians 2:12 tells us to work out our own salvation with fear and trembling. The words "work out" denotes a progressive work, not something immediately obtained. Part of us working out our own salvation is us submitting to the judgements of the Lord and allowing Him to abstract the iniquity in our life. All of this is imperative to our entry into the kingdom of God.

The Seed

"And I will put enmity between thee and the woman, and between thy seed and her seed; it shall bruise thy head, and thou shalt bruise his heel" (Genesis 3:15). The seed speaks of offspring. There's a war going on between the seed of the woman and the seed of the serpent. This statement was prophetic in nature. The seed of the woman would be a righteous nation (the Ekklesia) that would emerge in the image and likeness of God to destroy the darkness upon the earth. This started with Jesus and it continues with us today as the Ekklesia. What seed you are is determined by whose seed you have. I have mentioned this scripture quite a few times already, but I must address it again! This scripture is very important to your process and your progression in God. "He that committeth sin is of the devil; for the devil sinneth from the beginning. For this purpose the Son of God was manifested, that he might destroy the works of the devil.

Whosoever is born of God doth not commit sin; for his seed remaineth in him: and he cannot sin, because he is born of God. In this the children of God are manifest, and the children of the devil: whosoever doeth not righteousness is not of God, neither he that loveth not his brother" (1 John 3:8-10).

A life of sin makes you a child of the devil; when you refuse to allow God's processing to abstract the iniquity from your life then that makes you a child of the devil. If his seed is in you, then that makes you his seed (offspring); however if the seed of God remains in you after the seeds of the devil have been removed, then you are the seed of God. Galatians 3:16 says, "Now to Abraham and his seed were the promises made. He saith not, And to seeds, as of many; but as of one, And to thy seed, which is Christ." You are the seed of Abraham if you possess his seed (or the same seed Abraham had), which is Christ, the hope of glory. The promises of God are from the seeds of Abraham.

If you don't see the promises of God in your life, then it could be that you are of the wrong seed. Applying the principles of God and seeing results does not prove that you are the seed of God. The world can do this and see results! The promises are so much bigger than the application of principles. I may touch on this in another book, but this is something to meditate on.

There must be one seed that remains in you, which is the seed of God and of Christ. The reason why most believers war internally and struggle with the will of God is because the two seeds are at war with each other. Always remember that iniquity is a seed. The works of the flesh and other outward expressions of rebellion against the Father are fruits or manifestations of a seed of iniquity taking root and sprouting. Everyone is born with the seed of God in them. This is why most people have at least some sense of a moral code or knowing right from wrong.

As long as carnality or iniquity is present in a person's life then the seed of God will continue to be smothered. Carnality is the result of iniquitous seeds in a person. You can't have two seeds working in you and expect to be stable and receive the fullness of God. This is what causes one to be double minded and have double standards in God. You can't serve two masters nor can you be dominated by two seeds (read Matthew 6:24). It's either one or the other! Do you now see why submitting to proper processing and allowing the Lord to judge you is important? Without it, you will forfeit your inheritance.

Iniquity From the Tree

In the garden, there were two trees; the Tree of Life and the Tree of Knowledge of Good and Evil. Every human being is born and grows up with a sense of right and wrong. Even if they were not properly defined, we all have a sense of what is right and what is wrong. The right things, we have no problem doing out in the open. It's the wrong things that we sought to hide and do in secret because we did not want them to be found. In the beginning, God told Adam and Eve not to eat of the Tree of Knowledge of Good and Evil and to only eat from the Tree of Life. As long as he continued to eat from the Tree of Life, he could continue to enjoy the benefits of relationship and intimacy with the Father. Before Adam and Eve fell, the only seed in them was the seed of God. It was that seed that was supposed to be passed down generationally. When they ate of the tree of Knowledge of Good and Evil, that's when the seed of the devil entered into them and was passed to all humanity. When you know God personally, it's His holiness that sets you apart.

Without any knowledge of right or wrong, by just who He is, sets you apart when you seek Him and Him only. Relationship with God puts a distinction on you verses anything outside of God's realm. Adam and Eve did not need to know about good and evil because they knew God. Anything outside of that was foreign and wasn't desirable. When you are truly one with God, anything outside of His culture is not desirable. It's true relationship with God that makes you holy and separates you from evil. When you learn the nature and heart of God, anything outside of that is evil.

When they ate of the tree, knowledge of good and evil was passed to the succeeding generations. Where there was no temptation, now there is much temptation. The fruit of that tree immediately took them outside of God's realm and they became self conscious; however, this knowledge already existed in God. "And the LORD God said, Behold, the man is become as one of us, to know good and evil: and now, lest he put forth his hand, and take also of the tree of life, and eat, and live for ever" (Genesis 3:22). If Adam and Eve would have stayed in God, they would have known about good and evil, just from God's perspective. Because they sought this kind of revelation outside of God's realm, they became knowledgeable about good and evil through the lenses of their fall (self righteousness).

This is why the process is important! It takes you out of the fall and back into glory where Adam lived before he fell. Because of the fall, we have inherited the fruit and seeds from the Tree of Knowledge of Good and Evil, but thank God for Jesus who has given us access to the Tree of Life that keeps us grow in relationship with God. Relationship with God exposes us before God. It's the seed of iniquity that causes us to want to cover up our nakedness, just like Adam did. Adam tried to cover his nakedness when he crossed over to the knowledge realm. It's through exposure that we can actually be restored to paradise. He that has an ear, let him hear and understand!

The Benefit of Exposure

"Have mercy upon me, O God, according to thy lovingkindness: according unto the multitude of thy tender mercies blot out my transgressions. Wash me throughly from mine iniquity, and cleanse me from my sin. For I acknowledge my transgressions: and my sin is ever before me. Against thee, thee only, have I sinned, and done this evil in thy sight: that thou mightest be justified when thou speakest, and be clear when thou judgest. Behold, I was shapen in iniquity; and in sin did my mother conceive me. Behold, thou desirest truth in the inward parts: and in the hidden part thou shalt make me to know wisdom" (Psalm 51:1-6).

When it comes to iniquity we must understand and learn to appreciate the mercy of God. We must understand that God is not treating our offenses as they truly deserve. David understood the mercies of God. This Psalm was written when the prophet Nathan revealed David's transgression concerning him getting Uriah killed to take his wife Bathsheba. It wasn't until exposure came that he realized that he had a major issue. Many times exposure comes to open your eyes to the hidden iniquity inside of you. This is necessary because we do not always see ourselves correctly. David realized the presence of his iniquity, transgression, and sin. If you read verses ten through thirteen, you'll also see that David understood the severity of his iniquity. When iniquity is removed, then a recreation of your heart can take place.

God will create in you a clean heart when iniquity is removed. A right attitude and perspective will be formed along with that. If iniquity, transgression, and sin is not dealt with and removed from your life it can cause God's presence to leave you. Iniquity and transgression are major hindrances to the glory of God resting on your life. The reason why many believers cannot enjoy their salvation or a relationship with God is because many of them are full of everything that antagonizes your salvation and your relationship with God. This is why many believers look to the world for their enjoyment. Many of them are so full of iniquity that they can't enjoy the Lord, even if they tried.

Iniquity keeps you out of the Spirit. It's the seed either implanted in you from birth (which is most common) or what you have allowed to take root in you. It's designed to keep you from seeing and entering the kingdom of God. David recognized that his iniquity from birth contributed greatly to his transgression. This is bigger than demons or devils! Iniquity is the portal through which demons can enter. Flesh and demons are proof that iniquity is present. Iniquity keeps you imprisoned in the realm of your flesh. No matter how spiritual you try to be, you will always be drawn to make carnal decisions according to your mind and emotions. Even your opinion in spiritual matters will be corrupted! Iniquity keeps one focused on the world and it will seek to bring you into alignment with worldly or carnal standards. This is why it's important to submit to God's processing for your lives so we can truly experience the reality of the kingdom.

Chapter 8
The Kingdom Principles of Honor

When it comes to honor, many Christians fail in this area. It takes maturity to honor the right way. When honor is being taught in its proper context, many believers get uncomfortable because society has indoctrinated us to only honor the things and people that we like or are in agreement with. Honor has nothing to do with whether we agree, but has everything to do with the standard that God established before time began. Honor is an eternal principle that God originated. If you were to visit heaven, you would see a culture where people are honored not only for being a citizen of heaven, but also for their rank or function in the heavenly kingdom. Believe me when I tell you, when you die and go to heaven, you will not be floating around playing harps all day like it's depicted in cartoons on television. One thing I have learned from my process is how God truly feels about honor.

Honor opens the door for dominion and rulership. The reason why many believers do not experience breakthrough and advancement in their lives is because they choose not to honor. In the workplace dishonor will keep you stagnant, it will cause you to be overlooked in times of promotion, and will also cause you to get fired. Dishonor creates more losses and decreases than a million demons. We love to blame all of our woes and misfortunes on demonic activity. Even if there is demonic activity involved, I can guarantee you that dishonor opened the door to that activity. Much of the time, it is the act of dishonor itself that closes the right doors in our lives that need to be or should be open in our life. It is the acts of dishonor that causes God to overlook our time of promotion and gives it to another. Dishonor is very costly and the consequences of dishonor usually last a long time or even forever.

Honor is a Currency

We must understand that the kingdom of God is a kingdom of rewards. A "reward" is defined as: a recompense for efforts or services rendered. This system of reward in the kingdom of God can also be defined as a currency. "Currency" is defined as: transmission from person to person as a medium of exchange, a circulation. In the kingdom of God there is a currency that yields a system of reward in our lives. Faith is a currency. The bibles teaches us that God will reward us if we diligently seek Him in faith (read Hebrews 11:6). Another currency in the kingdom of God is honor for which there are rewards. Matthew 10:41 says, "He that receiveth a prophet in the name of a prophet shall receive a prophet's reward; and he that receiveth a righteous man in the name of a righteous man shall receive a righteous man's reward." If you don't receive and honor a vessel of God for who they are and what they possess in God, then you'll never see what they possess manifest in your life.

I can remember when I used to bash financial prosperity preachers. I got on the radio and talked about them really bad while I was broke and still believing God for my financial breakthrough. I know there are some who abuse these principles for selfish reasons, but that still doesn't change the fact that God wants us to financially prosper. It wasn't until I starting honoring and giving to those who successfully worked this principle, that I started seeing major financial increase in my life and ministry. What you honor, you will attract; you will see the same results as you apply similar principles. I've seen pastors dishonor the prophetic because of bad past experiences with prophets and now their ministry might as well be called "compromise city." The absence of a prophet will cause all kinds of breaches in a ministry and before you know it, all kinds of sin is permissible and accepted as normal. What you value will work for and will benefit you.

Those Who Love Are Those Who Honor

To honor means to value, esteem, appreciate, glory, give recognition, show gratitude, treasure, and consider precious. Anytime you're doing any one of these, you're honoring. On the contrary, dishonor means to treat something as common, lightly esteem, despise, and treat something as if it had little to no value. To receive honor in the kingdom of God, we must also give it. It's prideful and arrogant to believe that honor is owed when you refuse to give honor to whom it is due. It is a kingdom concept and if you don't understand it, then you don't understand the kingdom.

If you do not honor then you do not love. Love is the hallmark of spiritual maturity and love always honors. "Honour all men. Love the brotherhood. Fear God. Honour the king" (1 Peter 2:17). We see here that love and honor go hand in hand; without love you cannot honor. Honor causes you to see people in a different light. You need to see them the way God and heaven sees them. Love will cause you to see people through the lenses of the kingdom. "Be kindly affectioned one to another with brotherly love; in honour preferring one another" (Romans 12:10). Do you see that? Again, without love you cannot properly honor. People who do not honor are people who do not have the love of God in their hearts. These type of people are immature in the Lord; dishonorable people are immature people.

Whenever there is dishonor, there's a lack of love. A lack of love means there is a lack of character. A lack of character reveals a sign of immaturity. Immature believers have not been perfected in love. Everything we do must be motivated by love. The process of allowing God to truly judge our heart and character teaches us how to love. Even our faith must be motivated by love. "For in Jesus Christ neither circumcision availeth anything, nor uncircumcision; but faith which worketh by love" (Galatians 5:6). Our chastisement from God is motivated by love. "For whom the Lord loveth he chasteneth, and scourgeth every son whom he receiveth" (Hebrews 12:6). Our spiritual gifts must be used or desired with love (read 1 Corinthians 13; 14:1). So love is very vital to the Christian walk and we cannot properly honor without it.

Who Should be Honored

Who deserves honor? All men (read 1 Peter 2:17), civil authority and government (read Romans 13:1-8), natural parents (read Exodus 20:12, Ephesians 6:2), spiritual parents (read Ephesians 6:1), and other ministry leaders (read Matthew 10:40,41). You cannot honor God and not honor people. There are many people who claim to just honor God while dishonoring the people that He commands us to honor. This is wicked! To dishonor who God has honored is to dishonor God. "Wherefore the Lord God of Israel saith, I said indeed that thy house, and the house of thy father, should walk before me for ever: but now the Lord saith, Be it far from me; for them that honour me I will honour, and they that despise me shall be lightly esteemed" (1 Samuel 2:30). God honors those who honor Him. If you treat God common, then He'll treat you common. Could this be the reason your prayers are not getting answered? Could this be the reason you are sick? Could this be the reason you are financially broke? It's something to consider...

Familiarity Always Breeds Dishonor

"And he went out from thence, and came into his own country; and his disciples follow him. And when the sabbath day was come, he began to teach in the synagogue: and many hearing him were astonished, saying, From whence hath this man these things? and what wisdom is this which is given unto him, that even such mighty works are wrought by his hands? Is not this the carpenter, the son of Mary, the brother of James, and Joses, and of Juda, and Simon? and are not his sisters here with us? And they were offended at him. But Jesus, said unto them, A prophet is not without honour, but in his own country, and among his own kin, and in his own house. And he could there do no mighty work, save that he laid his hands upon a few sick folk, and healed them. And he marvelled because of their unbelief. And he went round about the villages, teaching" (Mark 6:1-6).

Jesus went among His own people who knew Him as a child. Their dishonor came because of familiarity; with whom you have become familiar, you will treat common. The people of his home town could not deny the wisdom and power of Jesus' ministry; however, they just couldn't get past the fact that they knew Him and His family. This is a classic sign of immaturity. Many times we miss God because we get too common with the one whom God has placed our answer in. The scriptures say that they were offended at him. People who are easily offended are usually dishonorable people. Those who are too familiar with you and want to see you as common are usually the ones who get offended when you obey God. They refuse to see you for who you are in God because they can't get past who you were or who they want you to be. Being easily offended or offensive always stems back to some type of dishonor and are major signs of immaturity.

Familiarity is the seed for dishonor. The people of Nazareth were so comfortable and common with the humanity of Jesus that they refused to accept His divinity. Familiarity will cause you to lose favor with God. When you dishonor who He has sent then you're dishonoring Him. God is always relational, but He's never common. Commonality puts two people on the same level and when it's present, familiarity has taken root. This is something that the body of Christ doesn't want to accept... No one is equal! There will always be someone who is superior to you. If you refuse to honor a superior in the kingdom of God, then you're dishonoring God's system of government that He has established. If you dishonor God's government, then you cannot receive from that government; you cannot be in the kingdom while dishonoring the kingdom.

"And he put forth a parable to those which were bidden, when he marked how they chose out the chief rooms; saying unto them. When thou art bidden of any man to a wedding, sit not down in the highest room; lest a more honourable man than thou be bidden of him; And he that bade thee and him come and say to thee, Give this man place; and thou begin with shame to take the lowest room. But when thou art bidden, go and sit down in the lowest room; that when he that bade thee cometh, he may say unto thee, Friend, go up higher: then shalt thou have worship in the presence of them that sit at meat with thee. For whosoever exalteth himself shall be abased; and he that humbleth himself shall be exalted" (Luke 14:7-11).

False entitlement is always a fruit of dishonor. In ancient society, the ranking protocol always required the best seat be given to the most eminent or highest ranking persons who often arrived last. If someone decides to get presumptuous or arrogant and decide to sit in the best seat (in front of everyone), this person would be told to head to the last seat. This is an open rebuke to prideful individuals who assumed preeminent status in priority and self importance. A dishonorable person will always prefer themselves above the ones who are ahead of them and paid the price to be where they are. The process always starts you at the bottom; God never starts someone at the top.

"A son honoureth his father, and a servant his master: if then I be a father, where is mine honour? and if I be a master, where is my fear? saith the Lord of hosts unto you, O priests, that despise my name. And ye say, Wherein have we despised thy name? Ye offer polluted bread upon mine altar; and ye say,

Wherein have we polluted thee? In that ye say, The table of the Lord is contemptible. And if ye offer the blind for sacrifice, is it not evil? and if ye offer the lame and sick, is it not evil? offer it now unto thy governor; will he be pleased with thee, or accept thy person? saith the Lord of hosts. And now, I pray you, beseech God that he will be gracious unto us: this hath been by your means: will he regard your persons? saith the Lord of hosts. Who is there even among you that would shut the doors for nought? neither do ye kindle fire on mine altar for nought. I have no pleasure in you, saith the Lord of hosts, neither will I accept an offering at your hand" (Malachi 1:6-10).

The priest dishonored God by not giving Him the best; they gave God a defected offering. What they were offering God, they wouldn't offer to a governor of the land. We as a church are guilty of treating civil and government authority better than we treat God and His kingdom. Many are guilty of treating their secular bosses and civil leaders better than they do the men and women of God. This is error! Even though the priest gave God gifts and an offering, they were defected. Gifts given in dishonor will not be accepted by the Lord. The Father knows who He is and what's entitled to Him. This is why regardless of your lack of understanding, He will not accept nothing less than what He deserves. Leaders take note! When you understand honor you will not allow the Lord to be treated any kind of way. You will also not allow yourself to be treated less than what God has placed on your life. If you have a problem with this statement, then you have a lot more maturing to do. Maturity seeks to give honor where it is due.

Honoring the Lord with the Best of Your Substance

"Honour the Lord with thy substance, and with the firstfruits of all thine increase: So shall thy barns be filled with plenty, and thy presses shall burst out with new wine" (Proverbs 3:9,10). "Substance" in Hebrew is the word "hon" (hone) and is defined as: wealth and riches. "Firstfruits" in Hebrew is the word “re shiyth” (ray-sheeth) and is defined as: first, beginning, best, chief, and choice part. This not only denotes priority, but it also is the best of what you have. "Increase" in Hebrew is the word “tebu ah” (teb-oo-ah) and is defined as: product, revenue, or income. We should honor God not just with our money, but the first and best parts of our money. People do not like when you talk about money, but you cannot properly honor without it.

People tend to give out of a need, instead of just honoring God. Some people will sacrifice when a need arises, but then they give God sloppy seconds. This is a major error in the church today and it shows how backwards our priorities are. This is why when people give or call themselves honoring, it yields little to no reward. There’s nothing wrong with expecting a return on what you give, but if you can’t give just to honor the Lord then you are indeed still immature in the faith. If the only time you give is when you need God to do something, then that demonstrates your lack of honor towards the Father. When you honor, you know God’s principles work; you don’t always look for something in return because you’re doing it out of love. We must seek to honor the Lord more financially; this will secure our finances so that the spirit of mammon cannot touch it.

Measures of Honor

“Look to yourselves, that we lose not those things which we have wrought, but that we receive a full reward” (2 John 1:8). If the bible says that there’s a full reward then that also means there is a partial reward. The measure in which you honor determines the measure of your reward. You receive full reward when you honor fully. If you don’t honor God by His standards and what’s due to Him, you won’t receive much from Him. The same thing goes with the men and women of God... you must honor them by God’s standards and not your own. It takes maturity to fully understand this.

There are different measures of honor; the same amount of honor is not due to everyone. Numbers 27:18-20 says, "And the Lord said unto Moses, Take thee Joshua the son of Nun, a man in whom is the spirit, and lay thine hand upon him; And set him before Eleazar the priest, and before all the congregation; and give him a charge in their sight. And thou shalt put some of thine honour upon him, that all the congregation of the children of Israel may be obedient." God told Moses to place SOME of his honor upon Joshua and because of this, all of Israel had to obey him. When it comes to a man or woman of God, the level of honor placed on them will determine your measure of obedience to them.

Everyone doesn't have the same measure of honor. Even secular society teaches us that! Joshua only received some of Moses' honor. Though He did what Moses couldn't, which was crossing the people over to the promise land, Joshua still wasn't greater than Moses. God did not initiate the covenant with Joshua, He initiated it with Moses; Joshua only carried on Moses' mandate to cross the people over into the promise. But without Moses, Joshua would not have had a government in God's kingdom. This proves that "greater works" doesn't mean "greater than." Joshua did what Moses could not do, but he wasn't greater than Moses.

Honor starts in the heart. The Holy Spirit said to me, "If you don't believe that the person you're honoring deserves the honor they're receiving, then your actions will eventually disprove your lip service." What's in the heart will eventually be revealed. "After this manner therefore pray ye: Our Father which art in heaven, Hallowed be thy name. Thy kingdom come, Thy will be done in earth, as it is in heaven. Give us this day our daily bread. And forgive us our debts, as we forgive our debtors. And lead us not into temptation, but deliver us from evil: For thine is the kingdom, and the power, and the glory, for ever. Amen" (Matthew 6:9-13).

The meaning of the word "hallowed" is: to honor as holy. So true holiness is directly linked to how you show honor. When you honor God properly, then you will treat Him like He's holy. Without honor you cannot access the rest of that passage. Without honor you cannot access the kingdom, revelation, forgiveness, deliverance, and the power and glory of God. I heard Apostle Guillermo Maldonado say this one day when he was teaching, "The problem is that we have replaced honor with faith. Your faith will not produce anything if you dishonor God. The area where you dishonor God in, your faith will not work." This saying is so true! God will never promote or increase you in dishonor. It's just like I mentioned earlier, when I dishonored those who taught biblical financial principles, (though I had faith for finances) I never saw it until I honored those principles and those who taught it. Even Jesus had to learn this!

"And the child grew, and waxed strong in spirit, filled with wisdom: and the grace of God was upon him. Now his parents went to Jerusalem every year at the feast of the passover. And when he was twelve years old, they went up to Jerusalem after the custom of the feast. And when they had fulfilled the days, as they returned, the child Jesus tarried behind in Jerusalem; and Joseph and his mother knew not of it. But they, supposing him to have been in the company, went a day's journey; and they sought him among their kinsfolk and acquaintance. And when they found him not, they turned back again to Jerusalem, seeking him. And it came to pass, that after three days they found him in the temple, sitting in the midst of the doctors, both hearing them, and asking them questions. And all that heard him were astonished at his understanding and answers. And when they saw him, they were amazed: and his mother said unto him, Son, why hast thou thus dealt with us? behold, thy father and I have sought thee sorrowing. And he said unto them, How is it that ye sought me? wist ye not that I must be about my Father's business? And they understood not the saying which he spake unto them. And he went down with them, and came to Nazareth, and was subject unto them: but his mother kept all these sayings in her heart. And Jesus increased in wisdom and stature, and in favour with God and man" (Luke 2:40-52).

Notice that even though God dealt with Jesus at an early age, He still had to be subject to Joseph and Mary. Jesus tried to start His ministry prematurely and in the process He operated in a spirit of dishonor. Yes... the Son of God made this mistake before He matured into His sonship with the Father. Instead of being submitted to His parents, Jesus got some revelation from the Father and thought that it was time to start His ministry. Though He had revelation, His immaturity caused Him to operate in a zeal that caused Him to dishonor the authority over Him (his parents). Jesus broke rank and dishonored His parents! This is why the Spirit of God did not come upon Him during this time. God will never honor anything initiated in the spirit of dishonor. Even the firstborn Son of God wasn't exempt from that! There are many ministries that have been erected in dishonor. Though there may be a movement, it's not the movement of the Spirit. When you choose to operate in dishonor, all you are left with is something familiar.

Honor Brings Promotion

Honor will cause you to be promoted in the lowest place of your life. Look at Joseph! If you study his life, you will see that though he was hated and betrayed by his own brothers, sold into slavery, subject to prison life, was falsely accused after refusing to sleep with Potiphar's wife, he still remained an honorable man. Consequently, his gift of interpreting dreams made room for him, brought him before royalty, and he was promoted second in command to the Pharaoh of Egypt. The same people who dishonored and betrayed him, were the ones who were subject to his mercy. Even in the midst of you being wronged, when you remain honorable the justice of God begins to rule in your favor and will cause you to rise above those who have made themselves an enemy to you.

Honor will always set you up for promotion no matter where or how you're positioned in life or ministry. In the low places of Joseph's life, because of his honor God promoted him to be above everyone else. He ended up being over everyone in the prison he was held captive in. So in his place of trial, betrayal, and despair, God still saw fit to promote Joseph because he understood the kingdom principle of honor. Promotion is inevitable when you learn to honor.

The Blessing, Honor, and Dominion

As stated previously, God honors those who honor Him (read 1 Samuel 2:30). This is very important to understand if we're going to walk in our true inheritance as believers. In the kingdom of God, in order to receive honor we first must give it.
"And when Abram was ninety years old and nine, the Lord appeared to Abram, and said unto him, I am the Almighty God; walk before me, and be thou perfect. And I will make my covenant between me and thee, and will multiply thee exceedingly. And Abram fell on his face: and God talked with him, saying, As for me, behold, my covenant is with thee, and thou shalt be a father of many nations. Neither shall thy name any more be called Abram, but thy name shall be Abraham; for a father of many nations have I made thee. And I will make thee exceeding fruitful, and I will make nations of thee, and kings shall come out of thee. And I will establish my covenant between me and thee and thy seed after thee in their generations for an everlasting covenant, to be a God unto thee, and to thy seed after thee" (Genesis 17:1-7).

The first thing we must recognize here is that God's covenant with Abram had conditions. God told Abram to "walk before me, and be thou perfect." Once he agreed to do this, then God would allow Abram to partake of the covenant and its benefits. Walking before God and being perfect is a way of honoring God with our lives. When we honor God with the way we live and walking upright before Him, then He'll honor us by allowing us to partake of the covenant that He made with our forefather Abraham. Last time I checked... we are the seed of Abraham by faith.

"There is neither Jew nor Greek, there is neither bond nor free, there is neither male nor female: for ye are all one in Christ Jesus. And if ye be Christ's, then are ye Abraham's seed, and heirs according to the promise" (Galatians 3:28,29).

"Not as though the word of God hath taken none effect. For they are not all Israel, which are of Israel: Neither, because they are the seed of Abraham, are they all children: but, In Isaac shall thy seed be called. That is, They which are the children of the flesh, these are not the children of God: but the children of the promise are counted for the seed" (Romans 9:6-8).

If we're in Christ, then we're Abrahams seed by faith and we're heirs of the promises of God made to Abraham. God told Abraham that royalty will come from his loins. I covered this subject previously, but I feel the need to address it again. Knowing this part of our inheritance is very important to our destiny. God's promise to Abraham always involved increase and dominion. When you truly honor God the way that He deserves to be honored, He will then increase you and cause you to have dominion. The same promise was made to Jacob.
"And God appeared unto Jacob again, when he came out of Padanaram, and blessed him. And God said unto him, Thy name is Jacob: thy name shall not be called any more Jacob, but Israel shall be thy name: and he called his name Israel. And God said unto him, I am God Almighty: be fruitful and multiply; a nation and a company of nations shall be of thee, and kings shall come out of thy loins" (Genesis 35:9-11).

When God decides to place honor upon your life, He changes your name or the way that you are identified; your identity changes when you enter into covenant with God. Notice that the blessing of God is linked to dominion, rulership, and kings. When God blessed Abraham and his descendants it was for the purpose of dominion. In Genesis 17:16, God told Abraham that He was going to bless his wife Sarah: she was going to be a mother of nations and that kings would come from her. In Genesis 1:28, God blessed them prior to instructing them to subdue the earth. To function in God's kingdom the way that you're designed to function, you first must be blessed by God. This is the same blessing that He would later bestow upon Abraham and his sons.

"Blessed" in Hebrew is the word "barak" and it means: to be adorned, kneel, to praise, and to salute. The Holy Spirit spoke to me while reading these definitions and He said, "These words are expressions of honor." To be blessed by God is to be honored by God. In order to receive the blessing from God we first must learn to honor Him with our life. Honor is also linked to worship. So when we learn to worship God with our life and not our lips, then we can receive the blessing from God. Salvation is free, but honor from God is earned. When God bestows honor upon you even the devil has to respect it!

The blessing of God was never given so that we can just acquire "stuff" - the blessing of God was given so that we can rule and have dominion. How do we receive honor? "The fear of the Lord is the instruction of wisdom; and before honour is humility" (Proverbs 15:33). "Before destruction the heart of man is haughty, and before honour is humility" (Proverbs 18:12). Before we can receive honor from God we first have to honor Him by submitting ourselves in total humility to Him. Also, we have to be honorable in our conduct with and before man. We have to honor those who God says to honor, in the way they're supposed to be honored. This is well pleasing to the Lord.

Honor and Riches

According to the bible, honor and riches are linked together. "Both riches and honour come of thee, and thou reignest over all; and in thine hand is power and might; and in thine hand it is to make great, and to give strength unto all" (1 Chronicles 29:12). "Wisdom and knowledge is granted unto thee; and I will give thee riches, and wealth, and honour, such as none of the kings have had that have been before thee, neither shall there any after thee have the like" (2 Chronicles 1:12).

"Therefore the Lord stablished the kingdom in his hand; and all Judah brought to Jehoshaphat presents; and he had riches and honour in abundance" (2 Chronicles 17:5).

"Riches and honour are with me; yea, durable riches and righteousness" (Proverbs 8:18).

"By humility and the fear of the Lord are riches, and honour, and life" (Proverbs 22:4).

By humility you obtain honor. Once you have received honor from the Lord, then the earth and it's resources will begin to work for you. The blessing of the Lord produces wealth in the life of the believer. Wealth and honor work together. We can't honor the Lord without our wealth and He can't honor us without His wealth and subjecting the resources of the earth to us. The poor were of the first people that Jesus came to preach the gospel to. "The Spirit of the Lord is upon me, because he hath anointed me to preach the gospel to the poor; he hath sent me to heal the brokenhearted, to preach deliverance to the captives, and recovering of sight to the blind, to set at liberty them that are bruised, To preach the acceptable year of the Lord" (Luke 4:18,19).

The word "poor" in Greek is the word “ptochos” and is defined as: being reduced to beggary, asking alms, destitute of wealth, influence, position, honor, and to be destitute in your spirit. Many times poverty is the result of the lack of honor; the answer to natural and spiritual poverty is the kingdom of God. When you honor God and the protocols of His kingdom, then wealth and riches should be your portion. According to Leviticus 25, the acceptable year of the Lord was originally called the year of Jubilee. It was a year of release from slavery, debt, obligation, and of restoration of lands to those who had sold them. In the Kingdom, when we honor God and He honors us, we’re released from everything that’s associated with lack and bondage. This is not an occasional event, but a way of life.

You can’t have dominion if you’re still subject to lack and bondage. We’re not bringing honor to God when we lack. 2 Corinthians 8:9 tells us that Jesus became poor to make us rich. This is both spiritually and naturally. Know that God wants you to be a recipient of honor in His kingdom! If you’re in Christ then you’re Abraham’s seed and an heir to the promise of honor and dominion that was given to him. We as believers must know our rights! Even though your full inheritance is not released to you until you’re matured (read Galatians 4:1,2), as a servant in the kingdom you’re still supposed to live well. If Solomon’s servants can live well (read 1 Kings 10:4,5), then those of us who serve in the kingdom of God can live well too. God has given us a way out of poverty and it’s through properly honoring Him, His principles, the men and women of God, and submitting to governing authority. This will get a person far in life and in the kingdom of God.

Lets make a practice of honor! I’m not just talking about before man, but in secret as well. Develop daily habits of honor. Start by honoring the Lord first in your time and priority. In doing this, now that you have this revelation, He can teach you how to properly honor. Honor shouldn’t just be an event, it should be a lifestyle. This is one of the major keys to seeing the kingdom active your life. There's no getting around it! We must honor God and those He says honor the way they're supposed to be honor. This is not idolatry, this is a commandment. God teaches us proper honor as we submit to the process.

Chapter 9
Submission to the Authority of the Kingdom

Any type of governmental institution has an authority structure that helps to maintain the culture and the order of that institution. In heaven, there is also an authority structure in place. If we're going to be in the kingdom of God we can't escape being submitted to God's authority structure in heaven and on earth. This is a touchy subject for a lot of people because society has indoctrinated us to rebel against authority... especially when we don't agree. This attitude is sinful and evil. God's kingdom is established on His authority and structure that He has put in place to keep everything balanced and in order.

God takes His authority structure very seriously, more seriously than we may realize. There are many people, especially Americans, that have a distorted view of freedom. Freedom doesn't mean anarchy. Freedom is not being able to do what your flesh wants to do; it is living by God's design and perfect system. This may be structured and the government may be weighty, but it is not overbearing and oppressive. Many people view submission and governance as oppressive and overbearing. This is far from the truth and until we decide to relinquish our will to God's will, we will never see it any other way.

Rebellion Against God's Authority

Lucifer, the anointed cherub, lost his position because he rebelled against authority. Pride and rebellion was the cause of his fall. Isaiah 14:12-15 and Ezekiel 28:13-17 describes his rise and fall; Isaiah tells us how he rebelled against God's authority and Ezekiel tells us how he rebelled against God's holiness. I submit to you today that the greater offense was against God's authority versus His holiness. Both are wrong, but offending God's authority carries a greater weight of judgement from Him, than offending His holiness. Look at Saul and David as an example. Both sinned against God, but the Spirit of God left Saul and stayed with David. David would go on to do many more sinful acts than Saul. Why was the Father harder on Saul? Because Saul sinned against God's authority by rebelling against a direct instruction from Him through Samuel.

When you rebel against a directive given by God's delegate in authority, you will bring a curse upon yourself. To offend the authority of God is far more offensive than offending His holiness. David offended God's holiness by getting Uriah killed on the frontline so that he could have Bathsheba to himself. Though David committed this sin he, was still considered to be a man after God's own heart. Why is that? I believe it's because He understood the severity of God's authority. This was why he never attempted to kill Saul even though Saul sought to kill him because of jealousy. Though Saul lost the presence of God in private, David still recognized the anointing on the public office as king and that Saul still had dominion as king. You don't lose dominion or authority because of sin. It takes maturity to understand and accept this. I know this will wreck a lot of folks religious theology, but God doesn't operate like man does.

As soon as a man of God makes a mistake we are the first ones to say "sit him down", "vote him out", or "I'm leaving." All of these responses are wicked, rebellious, and immature according to God's standards. The only way you lose dominion or your place of governance in God's kingdom is by death.

Adam lost dominion when he died and Saul was no longer king after his death. David didn't touch the Lord's anointed even though the Lord's anointed was wrong. In order to be a part of the move of God for our generation, you must understand this and govern yourself accordingly. True submission is when you can submit to an authority that you do not agree with.

This is where a lot of church people fall short. As soon as the man or woman of God falls in an area, we do just what Ham did when Noah was drunk... we broadcast their nakedness! We expose them instead of covering them. Noah cursed Ham's son, Canaan, because he offended God's authority. Noah was God's imperial authority in the earth during that time. God invested His authority in Noah and after his wrongdoing, that authority still remained. Noah had offended God's holiness by getting drunk, not His authority. Up until that time, Noah obeyed all of what God told him to do. He may have had an issue with his purity, but he was obedient to God.

This is why in Matthew 12:31 it records Jesus telling the Pharisees, "Therefore I say to you, any sin and blasphemy shall be forgiven people, but blasphemy against the Spirit shall not be forgiven." Why is this so? Because the Holy Spirit is the direct authority of the Godhead in the earth. He is the chief governor of all governors in the kingdom and He has senior ambassadorial rank in the kingdom of God. In Luke 12:10, it is stated that words against the Son of Man (Jesus) can be forgiven, but words against the Holy Spirit will not be forgiven. What we have to realize is that when this was written, Jesus Himself was under the authority of the Holy Spirit; He hadn't ascended to the right hand of the Father.

There was forgiveness for speaking against His humanity; this is why the phrase "Son of Man" was used. There would be no forgiveness for speaking against His divinity because that's where His authority came from. His authority came from who He was and His rank in the kingdom at that time. Immature people blaspheme the Holy Spirit easily because they use the humanity of a person to challenge their authority in God. This is wicked! This is why all of those who rejected him as the Son of God and the Messiah were judged. It's a sin to speak against the divine nature of God in a man.

This is why it's dangerous when you speak against a man's ministry because you disagree with some things about him naturally. Even when it comes to the manifestations of the Spirit, we're so quick to demonize what doesn't fit in our theology. This too is a blasphemous nature. If it clearly contradicts scripture then you can refute it, but if it's not refuted in scripture, even though it might not be mentioned verbatim then it's best to sit back and watch the fruit that it produces in the lives of people before judging it unrighteously. When you challenge the authority of a man or woman of God based upon natural flaws, what you dislike about them, a mistake they have made, or what you disagree with them about, you are blaspheming the Holy Ghost. Even if they are wrong, you cannot challenge or rebel against the government that is upon their life. What I am teaching in this book may not be popular, but it is kingdom.

Obedience to Authority

1 Peter 2:18 "Servants, be subject to your masters with all fear; not only to the good and gentle, but also to the froward." Your alignment with authority is more important than you being right. That right, you are reading this correctly! So many people are bent on proving that they are right when they feel that they have been wronged by authority, that they end up committing a greater sin by rebelling against the authority of God. In all that Saul was trying to do to David, David laid not one hand on him because he was still mature enough to recognize the authority of God invested in the office of the king that Saul occupied. David did not have kingship rank yet, so Saul's government was greater than his at that time. When

David fled for his life after Saul's attempt to kill him, he wasn't running from Saul. It was clear that He wasn't afraid of any man. David slew a lion, bear, and Goliath. David was fleeing from the authority of God invested in the office of kingship. He fled to keep from being put in a position to offend God's authority. Saul was a harsh leader, but David still had to honor his office and not rebel against his authority. "You must constantly remember your leaders, who spoke the Word of God to you, whose faith you must habitually imitate by observing carefully the result of their way of life... You must continually comply with your leaders and you must yield to them, for they keep watch over you as people who will given an account on behalf of your lives, and they could do this with joy if you do not complain: for this complaining is harmful to you" (Hebrews 13:7,17 *ONMB*).

This says to constantly remember your leaders. "Remember" is defined as: emphasizing the importance of what is asserted, to call to mind. We're to constantly remember our leaders and the authority they have in our lives, and imitate their faith in God. The next verse says we're to continually comply with our leaders. "Comply" is defined as: an act in accordance with a wish or command. It is synonymous with the words obey, adhere to, conform to, follow, and respect. So we're to constantly obey our leaders. There's no getting around that command in scripture. All authority is instituted by God and all authority requires obedience; immature Christians are quick to rebel against set authority.

Men should obey delegated, civil (read Romans 13:1-8 and 1 Peter 2:13,14), and especially spiritual authority. The only time authority is not to be obeyed is when they tell you to do something that's clearly against what's already written in scripture. Parents: if you don't obey the authority of God in your life, then don't expect your children to obey you. When you're rebellious, that gives rebellion a legal right to rule your house and to rule the ones you're supposed to rule.

"Children, obey your parents in the Lord: for this is right. Honour thy father and mother, (which is the first commandment with promise)" (Ephesians 6:1,2). Notice it says to obey your parents in the Lord (spiritual parents) and it says to honor your father and mother. Spiritual parents are to be obeyed while natural parents are to be honored. Many may have a hard time swallowing this pill, but it's clear in scripture! I'm talking about grown adults! If we're going to believe the word then we need to believe the whole word and stop skipping over the parts that we don't agree with! Prison, the unemployment line, grave, and Hell are all full of people who rebelled against authority. Rebellion will always put you in some type of bondage and place you under some type of curse. Rebellion is the sin unto death. Only rebels look for excuses not to obey authority.

There's No Grace for Rebels

We must understand that to rebel against God's delegated authority is to rebel against God. "Indeed when we are sinning deliberately after taking the knowledge of the truth, no further offering remains concerning sins, but some fearful expectation of judgment with its blazing flames appears like a living being intent on devouring God's adversaries. Anyone who has set aside the Torah (Teaching) of Moses dies without pity on the testimony by two or three witnesses: (Deut. 17:6; 19:15) how much more worthy of punishment do you suppose the one will be who trod down the Son of God and who looked upon the blood of the covenant, by Whom he was sanctified, as defiled, and has insulted the Spirit of Grace" (Hebrews 10:26-29 *ONMB*).

To do something deliberately after knowing it's wrong in God's eyes is called rebellion. Rebellion is when you do the opposite of what God says do. Rebellion is equivalent to insulting the Spirit of Grace, consequently there is no grace for rebellion. It automatically places you under the judgement of God. We can clearly see that the blood of Jesus doesn't atone for rebellion. There's no more sacrifice or offering for your sins when you're in rebellion. This is why this is the sin unto death; you are spiritually dead and cut off from God. Rebellion is something that you don't get delivered from. You have to consciously come out of agreement with it by submitting yourself to the judgements of God.

When you rebel, you're already under judgement. You might as well submit and let it purify you! If you don't allow the judgements of God to purify you, then it will eventually destroy you. In verse 28, it tells us that those who rebelled against the law of Moses died without mercy on the testimony of two or three witnesses. I want you to notice that it says the laws or teachings of Moses. Why is it called the law of Moses instead of the law of God? I believe it's because God uses people to execute his will and He never separates the work from those He's given charge over the work.

In Numbers 16, two hundred and fifty leaders of the congregation gathered together against Moses and Aaron, and Korah was the head of that company. Moses and Aaron were told that they take too much upon themselves and that they shouldn't lift themselves up over the assembly because everyone was holy and that God is among everyone. We all know how that ended! Korah, his family, and his company were swallowed when the earth opening up to consume them; everyone else who agreed with Korah was consumed by fire.

These people thought that they were just rebelling against Moses and Aaron. They weren't trying to rebel against God directly, but failed to realize that God never separates himself from those He delegates authority to; God and His delegated authority are inseparable. The attitude towards Moses and Aaron was an attitude towards God.

Lets examine the account in Numbers 12 when Aaron and Miriam rebelled against the authority of Moses because they didn't like his decision to marry an Ethiopian woman. Their opinion concerning his personal life caused them to dishonor the authority and rank Moses walked in. I want you all to keep a mental note of this. How you feel about your leader's personal life and decisions is irrelevant to the fact that God has called you to submit to His authority upon their life. You may not agree, but look at what happened to Miriam as a result of this same action.

When Aaron and Miriam attempted to question Moses' personal decision, God asked them were you not afraid to speak against my servant Moses? He was the faithful in all of the Lord's house. He was more faithful than they were. You don't mess with a man that's faithful to God even if you feel like they're wrong. If they're truly faithful to God then they will hear God when He corrects them in their wrong. God has not called us to police our leadership, He has called us to submit to their leadership.

Lets look at Nadab and Abihu in Leviticus 10:1,2 (*ONMB*), "And Nadab and Abihu, the sons of Aaron, each of them took his fire-pan and put fire in it and put incense on it, and offered strange fire before the Lord, which He commanded them not to do. And fire went out from the Lord and devoured them, and they died before the Lord." God never meant for Nadab and Abihu to serve independently from the leadership of Aaron their father. In Leviticus 9, we see Aaron making the sacrifices with his sons assisting him. The sons were never supposed to do this by themselves apart from Aaron. They probably meant well in their heart, but they were still destroyed. Why? Because they rebelled against God's authority which at that time was Aaron under Moses. They thought they could serve apart from the oversight or authority of Aaron. This is what strange fire is - serving without being submitted to or properly aligned with authority. This is what causes judgment to be put on many people in the church today.

In Genesis 9:20-27, we read where Noah was drunk in his tent naked and went to sleep. When Ham discovered his father's nakedness instead of covering him up, he went to his brothers to expose his father's nakedness. This was a spirit of dishonor in action. In other inspired writings during that time, it was said that Noah had a garment that was passed all the way down from Adam to him, and Ham stole that too. This was why Noah cursed his son Canaan. Does it seem like everything you do or everything that you're try to produce is falling apart? I can guarantee you that it's connected in some way to an act of dishonor towards an authority figure or a previous authority figure in your life. What Ham produced (his son, Canaan) got cursed because of his dishonor and dishonesty and God never told Noah he was wrong for cursing him.

We Are Gods

"And the Lord said unto Moses, See, I have made thee a god to Pharaoh: and Aaron thy brother shall be thy prophet" (Exodus 7:1). Did you just read that? The Lord made Moses a god to Pharaoh. I know some folks are probably looking crossed eyed right now, but this is what scripture says! God gave Moses power of attorney to not only act on His behalf, but to act as Him in the earth. Moses was not Jehovah; however He was authorized by Jehovah to be the direct reflection of His person and authority in the earth. This is also true regarding authentic apostolic leadership or those who possess imperial authority in the earth. One of the meanings of the Greek word "apostolos" is power of attorney. This gives you the authority to act on behalf of and as the individual you're representing. In this case, it's the Father that the apostle is representing in this manner. For those who are stuck at the god part... Here's what Psalm 82:6 says, "I have said, Ye are gods;

and all of you are children of the most high." Being a god and a child of God goes hand in hand.

Jesus makes a reference to this scripture in John 10:33-38 *ONMB*, let's go there..."The Jewish leaders answered Him, We are not stoning You concerning good works but concerning blasphemy, and because You are a man although You are making Yourself God." Y'shua answered them, "Has it not been written in your Torah (Teaching) that 'I said, you are gods?' (Ps. 82:6) If He called those gods to whom the Word of God came, then the Scripture cannot be done away with. Are you saying to the One Whom the Father sanctified and sent into the world, that 'You are blaspheming,' because I said, 'I am a Son of God'? If I do not do the works of My Father, do not believe Me: but if I am doing the works, even if you would not believe in Me, believe in the works, so that you would know and you would continue knowing that the Father is in Me and I am in the Father."

Being a god and being a child of God are synonymous. What does it truly mean to be a child of God? It means to be an offspring of someone and if you are a true offspring, then you will have a similar genetic makeup as the one who sired you. This is not in the context of maturity even though you do have to be mature to represent God on this level. This has to do with being a direct offspring of the Father. You're no longer just a creation, you're genetically identical to the Father in every way. So if you are truly a child of Jehovah God then that makes you a god, and if you are a god, then you would do the works of Jehovah God your Father. We as a church are so beneath the standards of God and His kingdom, it's sad. We would rather believe that we're nothing, than to just accept what our Father clearly says about us.

All of us are supposed to reach godlike status, but the sad reality is that most believers never reach that place in God. They still embody the genetic makeup of their past life before

Christ. Most believers have come to accept the nature of Adam's fall instead of the new nature that's available in Christ. There are those who reach this status in God by their love and obedience towards Him. Though Moses was flawed in certain areas, His heart was upright before God. When God elevates a man and gives him power then you must honor that. Moses was a god to the people and the people either honored him or were judged very harshly for rebelling against him. This can also be true even in a godly marriage. Wives are commanded to submit to their husbands as unto the Lord (read Ephesians 5:22). This means that the wife submits to the husband in the same way she would submit to the Lord. The voice of your husband is equal to the voice of God in your marriage when the husband is rightly positioned. The husband is the god / lord of his household under Jesus; the husband is the god / lord of his wife. Some of the most powerful women I've ever met are those who submit to their godly husbands in this manner. This is why it's important to marry the right person.

Those who rebel against God's authority are not in the kingdom of God. God's kingdom is established on His authority and He delegates that authority to those He wishes. We can't change God's rules because we don't like them. If we don't like what God has established then it just shows how far away from God we really are. You are not obedient to God if you're rebellious against the man or woman of God. Alignment with God's earthly delegated authority determines your standing with Him. Remember, God always uses man to execute His intention even in the lives of other people. Though we're not called by man, we're still commissioned by man. Rebellion against a set leader in your life will prevent God from allowing that leader to commission you.

Believe it or not, submission and humility is the only way up. The only way to reach high places in God is to first take the low road. When you take the road towards humility and total submission, then you become teachable enough to be discipled in higher realms and levels of knowledge and revelation in the Lord. God exalts the humble in their due season (read Matthew 23:12; 1 Peter 5:6; James 4:10). God gives grace to the humble (read James 4:6). Healing and forgiveness of sin are given to those that are humble (read 2 Chronicles 7:14). There are so many more scriptures on the subject of humility. Find those scriptures, study them, master them, and see how your natural and spiritual life will be transformed through constant application.

Authority is important to God because it comes from Him. Everything established by God is important. Many people would love to dismiss everything I'm saying in this book by saying that it's not important and we just need to win souls… HaHa! How can we win souls and then bring them into something God never ordained or that is totally contrary to His system of governance? The kingdom of God is not just about winning souls! The kingdom and the Ekklesia is a government before it's anything else. We can't skip the governmental function and think that we are in perfect standing. In this season, we have to fully embrace the governmental identity of the kingdom of God. We have to honor all of what He establishes, not just the parts we're comfortable with.

Chapter 10
The Fathering Model of the Kingdom

We cannot fully mature without understanding spiritual fathering. To see God's original intent for the fathering model, we need to go back to the beginning. Many have a problem with acknowledging another father other than their natural father, but as we will see, spiritual fathering is a biblical concept.

"And God said, Let us make man in our image, after our likeness: and let them have dominion over the fish of the sea, and over the fowl of the air, and over the cattle, and over all the earth, and over every creeping thing that creepeth upon the earth. So God created man in his own image, in the image of God created he him; male and female created he them" (Genesis 1:26-27).

We have to remember that Adam was the first father on earth and is father of all mankind. God the Father blessed Adam before He commanded increase from him. The blessing from a real father will always put a demand for increase and multiplication upon your life. Any man who claims to be your father and is not concerned with your growth and increase, does not have the heart of a father. God is the father of Adam and Eve and His blessing upon their life caused increase. The blessing of the Father also demands generational increase and dominion; Adam was charged to reproduce Jehovah's DNA in the earth. Today (after the new covenant) this happens through discipleship from a real father in the Lord. Multiplication is about making disciples.

There's a difference between being taught and being discipled. Someone may be able to teach or instruct you pertaining to a certain subject, but they may not be able to oversee your succession in what you have been taught. Many times they may only be able to go a certain distance with you. I believe this is why many people get disappointed in ministry and with those they submit to as spiritual fathers. They hook up with leaders who may have great revelation or walk in great power with the Lord, but they're not graced to go the distance with them. Disappointment sets in when expectations are not met and then a feeling of being hurt. When God allows leaders to pour into us, we must make sure that we properly discern their measure of leadership in our lives. If we keep our relationships before the Lord, then we can eliminate much of the hurt that results from being disappointed. Teachers instruct, but fathers have the grace to disciple you into your destiny.

The Difference Between Instructors and Fathers

"I write not these things to shame you, but as my beloved sons I warn you. For though ye have ten thousand instructors in Christ, yet have ye not many fathers: for in Christ Jesus I have begotten you through the gospel. Wherefore I beseech you, be ye followers of me. For this cause have I sent unto you Timotheus, who is my beloved son, and faithful in the Lord, who shall bring you into remembrance of my ways which be in Christ, as I teach every where in every church" (1 Corinthians 4:14-17).

There are many who try to refute the spiritual fathering model of ministry, but the Apostle Paul made reference to it often in scripture. You must know the difference between an instructor and a father. An instructor will impart knowledge pertaining to a particular subject, but it's your father who you are supposed to be imitate with in the faith. "Instructor" in Greek is the word “paidagogos” (pahee-dag-o-gos), which is defined as: a tutor, a guardian, and a guide of boys. Among the Greeks and Romans, this name was applied to trusted slaves who were charged with the duty of supervising the life and morals of boys that belonged to an upper class; before manhood, boys were not allowed to leave the house without their instructors. An instructor will lead and guide you until you reach maturity.

Instructors will be outgrown. Similarly to a school teacher when you pass their class, you move on to the next grade and will most likely have a different instructor. On the contrary, you will never outgrow a father and will always possess his DNA; your father will always be a part of you. Your genetics will bear the record of their faith in God imparted into you to move in greater things. In Greek, "Father" is the word “pater” (pat-ayr) and is defined as a generator; a generator is someone or something that produces and deals with the source of something. Paul told the Church at Corinth, “I am your source, I am your generator, because I have begotten you through the gospel." God uses your natural father to produce you in the earth, He also uses your spiritual father to give you placement and identity in the Kingdom.

Fathers disciple you into the fullness of God's kingdom. Paul said, “I have begotten you through the gospel." Begotten means to be born or formed through a process. What the Apostle Paul was saying here is that he was the one qualified to be their father because he formed them through a process. He labored in discipleship with the people until Christ was formed in them. This denotes paying attention to the details of your heart's condition and your walk with God. Instructors are graced for what you learn; however, fathers are graced for who you are and your development as a man or woman of God. Both are needed and can be essential to your walk with the Lord, but you must determine by the Spirit who is who.

Truly Being Born Again

Now what I'm about to say is going to be controversial and I won't be surprised if I get persecuted for it! We must understand that though God is sovereign, He executes His intentions in the earth through man. This is something that we must always keep in mind. He doesn't exclude man in anything that He does, including the redemptive work of His people on the earth. Though redemption was at the cross, many have still not entered into the reality of what has been made available as a result. God uses men and women to demonstrate the reality of what Jesus did on the cross, and the reality of His resurrection.

"He that committeth sin is of the devil; for the devil sinneth from the beginning. For this purpose the Son of God was manifested, that he might destroy the works of the devil. Whosoever is born of God doth not commit sin; for his seed remaineth in him: and he cannot sin, because he is born of God. In this the children of God are manifest, and the children of the devil: whosoever doeth not righteousness is not of God, neither he that loveth not his brother" (1 John 3:8-10).

If you read the entire chapter of 1 John 3 in context, you'll see that it's pertaining to sonship with God and the hallmarks of one who is truly born again as a son of God. The scriptures are clear on what a born again believer looks like. If you're truly born of God, you cannot sin because the seed of God in you forbids you to do so. This clearly shows us what a true born again son of God looks like. It's alarming that the Church has fallen so short in this area! I would dare say that most of the church is not born again, but are riding off of the fumes of grace. The purpose of the work of Christ is to destroy sin in our lives. While we're making excuses for our sin, the above scripture eliminates our excuses. As long as sin reigns in your life, then you are not completely born again. "Jesus answered and said unto him, Verily, verily, I say unto thee, Except a man be born again, he cannot see the kingdom of

God... Jesus answered, Verily, verily, I say unto thee, Except a man be born of water and of the Spirit, he cannot enter into the kingdom of God" (John 3:3,5).

Paul said he had begotten his spiritual children through the gospel (read 1 Corinthians 4:15). The word "begotten" is paternal language and deals with the process of conception and development until birth. Remember, when the Father does anything in the earth pertaining to His work in our lives, it is mostly accomplished through a human vessel. I submit to you that once you're truly begotten, then you're able to be born again. You cannot become born again all by yourself! Repeating a prayer doesn't make you born again! Becoming born again is a process that only the grace of God and a spiritual father can see you through. You are not born again until your parents in the Lord birth and form you through a process; this is to totally deliver you from the dominion of darkness. Spiritual fathers play a major role in this process by being graced to form and prepare you for delivery into the new world, the new Jerusalem, the kingdom of God.

If you're not born again, you will not see the Kingdom nor will you see it in your life. You must be born of water and spirit. Being born of water is having a personal revelation of the King and His kingdom. It is not through reading a book or watching videos, but through a growing relationship with God. This is a place of illumination and enlightenment. You'll even begin to discover who you are in God and who you are in His kingdom. Ephesians 5:26 talks about the washing of water by the word. In Greek, "word" is the word "rhema" which is defined as: what God is currently speaking at the moment or a "right now" prophetic revelation. Being born of water is being immersed or birthed into a whole new reality of revelation concerning the King and the kingdom of God. Water is a cleanser and a thirst quencher. When you get to this place of enlightenment, all of what you desire internally will be satisfied.

When you're born of the spirit, your life is governed by Him. Romans 8:14 says, "for as many as are led by the Spirit of God, they are the sons of God." "Sons" is a paternal word, so you are not a son of God nor do you possess His DNA if you are not led by the Spirit. Being led by the Spirit in all things means that you are born again and are immersed in the reality of His spirit. Sin cannot rule where His Spirit resides and governs. God's spirit must be able to have a permanent habitation in your life. When you are born again, there is no sin to grieve His Spirit.

Christ Being Formed in You

"My little children, of whom I travail in birth again until Christ be formed in you" (Galatians 4:19). You can clearly see the paternal language in this scripture. Paul felt the spiritual birth pain (suffering and labor) of birthing his sons and daughters. He suffered for the sake of their spiritual development and translation into the kingdom of God. It takes the labor and the process of your spiritual father for Christ to be formed in you. Forming denotes a process of development. Anything that has to be developed takes a period of time to enter into full maturity. A mentor is not graced to go to this depth with you.

"Now I say, That the heir, as long as he is a child, differeth nothing from a servant, though he be lord of all; But is under tutors and governors until the time appointed of the father" (Galatians 4:1-2). The time of maturity is appointed by the father, not the mentor. A mentor may mature you in a certain subject and form good qualities in you, but your father is graced to mature and form Christ in YOU. Only a father can measure your full maturity in God versus your maturity pertaining to a certain subject; your maturity is measured by how much of Christ is formed in you. When Christ is completely formed in you, you will exemplify all of his characteristics. In the kingdom of God your maturity is not measured by your age, but by your love walk and the characteristics of Christ being demonstrated through you. Fathers form your character by taking you through a process.

Fatherlessness Brings a Curse

"Behold, I will send you Elijah the prophet before the coming of the great and dreadful day of the Lord: And he shall turn the heart of the fathers to the children, and the heart of the children to their fathers, lest I come and smite the earth with a curse" (Malachi 4:5-6). The absence of a father brings the presence of a curse. The word "curse" in Hebrew is the word "charam" (khaw-ram) which means: to prohibit, to put under a ban (legal prohibition, block, forbid, disallow, suppress), and to dedicate for destruction. "Father" in Hebrew is the word "ab" which is defined as: head or founder of a household, group, family, or clan, generator, chief. What is God saying? He's saying He would send the spirit of Elijah to restore the spiritual father and son model to the people of God. He is connecting His people back to their "spiritual" source, not heavenly source (God), but spiritual source in their spiritual fathers.

Abraham is the father of all earthly fathers because it's through him that we're able to receive the promises of God that were given to him through his lineage. We are of his lineage by faith in Jesus Christ (read Galatians 3:7). When the presence and influence of a father is absent, legal bans and prohibitions are present, preventing further advancement in the perfect will of God. Without the presence of fathers to set standards and boundaries, children tend to run wild doing their own thing, all in the name of Jesus. Nearly 2 out of 5 children in America do not live with their fathers. What runs rampant in society is reflected by what is either allowed or ignored in the Church. The reason there's a lack of fathering in society is because there's a lack of fathering in the Church.

"And God wrought special miracles by the hands of Paul: So that from his body were brought unto the sick handkerchiefs or aprons, and the diseases departed from them, and the evil spirits went out of them. Then certain of the vagabond Jews, exorcists, took upon them to call over them which had evil spirits the name of the Lord Jesus, saying, We adjure you by Jesus whom Paul preacheth. And there were seven sons of one Sceva, a Jew, and chief of the priests, which did so. And the evil spirit answered and said, Jesus I know, and Paul I know; but who are ye? And the man in whom the evil spirit was leaped on them, and overcame them, and prevailed against them, so that they fled out of that house naked and wounded" (Acts 19:11-16).

The seven sons of Sceva tried to imitate the ministry of Apostle Paul because they saw high level demons responding to his authority. When you try to imitate the ministry of a man of God that you do not honor or are not submitted to, it's not likely that you will get the same results. The people that were receiving the miracles and deliverances were ones who practiced witchcraft and black magic (read Acts 19:19). The seven sons of Sceva were known exorcists and vagabonds; they had a traveling deliverance ministry. It's evident that they had some type of results in expelling demons because in the scriptures, they were called exorcists. They were fathered in the natural, but were bastards in the spirit and in ministry. Let me show you this curse at work...

When they attempted to mimic the deliverance ministry of Apostle Paul, the demons recognized that they were beyond their jurisdiction and were uncovered. The seven sons were dealing with very high level occult demons that they were not graced for; they were successful at dealing with low level demons, but they were outranked! Because they couldn't cast out these high level demons and were overpowered by them is evidence that the curse was at work. The curse that was spoken of in Malachi was a legal ban, a prohibition, a suppressing, and a blockage. They couldn't advance any further in the realm of deliverance because the grace from an apostolic father was absent. Naturally, fathers prepare you for life. In the Kingdom, fathers prepare you for ministry and living in the supernatural reality of the kingdom of God, and prepare you for destiny. A gift can only take you so far... you need to be properly developed and formed through a process (begotten). When you refuse the voice and influence of a father in your life, you inherit a curse causing you to never reach your full potential in the kingdom of God.

Loss and defeat is inevitable when you ignore the voice of a father. In 1 Samuel 15, we can recall the account of Saul being rejected as king because of rebellion and stubbornness. In verse 1, Samuel made it clear where His kingship came from and who God used to bestow it upon him; it was through Samuel's anointing and impartation. Samuel was a father to Saul and the instructions of the Lord came through him. When Saul rebelled against the instructions, he lost the glory of God.

In verse 23, Saul was rejected by God as king and his kingship was passed to another. When you're rebellious and stubborn against spiritual authority and fathering, you allow yourself to be put in a position where your destiny can be forfeited, and passed to another.

Another example of this is when the kingdom was passed from the Jews to the Church (read Matthew 21:43). In this passage, Jesus was speaking to the chief priests and the Pharisees. The Kingdom was taken from them and given to the Church (which consisted of Jew and Gentile believers in Jesus). They claimed that Abraham was their father (naturally and in the faith), but refused to accept Jesus as the One sent from God even though His works proved it. Because they rejected Jesus, He became a stumbling stone. When you reject truth, that truth becomes a stumbling stone... somebody will catch that next week! In John 8:56, Jesus said, "your father

Abraham rejoiced to see my day: and he saw it, and was glad." The same father (Abraham) whom they proudly claimed, also foreseen Jesus' ministry on the earth. The Pharisees were so blind (by choice) that they couldn't see that Jesus was the fulfillment of the promise made to their "father" Abraham. Abraham was their father naturally, but he wasn't their father in the faith, and neither was God. When you refuse to recognize a genuine son of God then you don't know God, and He's not your Father. When you reject someone who carries the DNA of the Father, then you're rejecting the Father.

The Real Seed of Abraham

In John 8, there is a dialog between Jesus and the Pharisees; the Pharisees were arguing about being the seed of Abraham, but Jesus redefined the meaning of "seed." We must understand that lineage is important to God and to the advancement of the kingdom. It insures the continuum of what God has released in the earth throughout all generations. The bible is full of different accounts of genealogical records. Lineage is important for securing and passing on a legacy. Even though the people of Israel were the natural descendants of Abraham, Jesus clearly communicated to the Pharisees that they were not the children of Abraham. In John 8:39 Jesus said, "if you were Abraham's children, you would do the works of Abraham." Then He said in verse 44, "ye are of your father the devil, and the lust of your father ye will do..."

Jesus redefined the meaning of being a seed or offspring. Who's son you are is determined by whose example you follow. Whoever you pattern yourself after and whose faith you imitate reveals what lineage you come from. Your natural lineage doesn't count when it comes to your placement in the kingdom of God. The Pharisees kept putting emphasis on their natural lineage as justification of where they thought they were in the kingdom. On the other hand, Jesus put more emphasis on the example or pattern that is followed to prove the identity of your real father.

Because God nor Abraham was their real Father, they became unworthy of the kingdom of God, it was stripped from them, and given to the Church. The Pharisee refused to follow the example of a true father in the faith and were blinded to the presence of the kingdom. Hear me in the spirit! They could not enter into the kingdom and also prevented others from entering (read Matthew 23:13).

Honor Comes From a Father

God uses fathers to bestow honor upon their sons. In John 8:54 Jesus said, "if I honour myself, my honour is nothing: it is my Father that honoureth me...." When you decide to bestow honor upon yourself, it carries absolutely no weight in the kingdom of God. Real honor can only come from a father; someone who is qualified to beget you (through a process) in the kingdom. "And the Lord said unto Moses, Take thee Joshua the son of Nun, a man in whom is the spirit, and lay thine hand upon him; And set him before Eleazar the priest, and before all the congregation; and give him a charge in their sight.And thou shalt put some of thine honour upon him, that all the congregation of the children of Israel may be obedient" (Numbers 27:18-20).

I covered this verse before, but I need to cover it again in the context of fathering. We see that honor was placed upon Joshua through the laying on of hands from his father Moses. It was because of this honor that all of Israel was commanded to obey Joshua. For the record, you're not authorized to obey anyone who has not received proper impartation of honor from a spiritual father; this is the proper way to receive honor from God in the kingdom. Impartation through a father will catapult you past limitations and barriers set up against your assignment, and thrust you beyond where your father has been. Elijah and Elisha are a perfect example of this. The scriptures record that Elisha did twice as many miracles as his father Elijah. The curse of limitations, bans, suppression, blockages, and such things alike are broken through proper impartation of honor from a genuine father.

Expansion From Headship

When it comes to spiritual fathering, we must understand the purpose of it. When God blessed Adam and Eve by telling them to be fruitful, multiply, and have dominion, it was for the purpose of preservation and expansion. The garden was made for man to thrive in. If we look at the word "garden" in Hebrew, it is the word "gan" and is defined as: enclosure (an area that is sealed off with an artificial or natural barrier). The garden was a divine encasement, an enclosed atmosphere of the supernatural reality of the kingdom of God; Adam and Eve were supposed to grow their family in this atmosphere and reality. In their multiplication, the enclosure was to become so populated that it couldn't contain all of their sons and daughters, eventually forcing them to expand. The spiritual fathering model is always for expansion and advancement. It's not to lord over a bunch of people and keep them under you. You should want the seed of God that has been placed in you to be imparted into those who follow you.

Another thing we have to understand is that God doesn't do everything through everyone. When God wants to initiate something, He does not gather a bunch of people and then place a leader over them. God starts with a man first and then increases multitudes to follow that man. God always expands from headship, not the other way around. That is the God model of leadership and the order of the kingdom. He does not entrust everything to everyone! He finds one who is faithful and preordained to lead and multiplies from that individual. The move always starts with one man no matter how many people are a part of it. God ordains one man to spearhead the move and from that one man authority is delegated. Many don't like it, but this is God's way.

Measuring Maturity

The spiritual son must realize that their spiritual inheritance and destiny is locked inside the loins of their spiritual father. At the right time appointed of the father, impartation comes for greater advancement and assuming greater responsibility in the kingdom of God. "Now I say, That the heir, as long as he is a child, differeth nothing from a servant, though he be lord of all; But is under tutors and governors until the time appointed of the father" (Galatians 4:1-2).

Fathers have grace to measure your maturity. Your maturity level dictates your divine appointment for the current season. It's necessary that fathers measure your maturity level so that you won't enter into major responsibility prematurely. A son released prematurely can be devastating to the body of Christ and is also dangerous for the son. "An inheritance may be gotten hastily at the beginning; but the end thereof shall not be blessed" (Proverbs 20:21). A son released too late can cause someone's destiny to be postponed or to miss God. The grace of a father in measuring maturity is needed so that the body of Christ can move into greater dimensions of faith and glory. It's also needed so that the people of God can move in God's correct timing for their lives. This will secure the advancement of the kingdom in future generations.

Fatherlessness Causes a Decline in Apostolic Power

There are many things that the church has lost over the previous centuries because the presence of genuine apostolic fathers began to die off. During the rule of Emperor Constantine and the dark ages immediately following, is where we saw a major decline in the presence of apostolic fathers and the revelation that they brought to the Church. When Constantine sought to “christianize” Rome, he removed apostolic and prophetic authority, power, presence, and function from the church and changed it’s governance to a board of pastors and bishops. This is the origin of our modern church structure and where we get church boards from today. He took out the ones who had the actual grace to father causing a false fathering model to be put in place. This false model is demonstrated through hierarchies that are unbiblical in scripture, oppressed servitude, ungodly submission to tyranny, and the adoption of pagan customs. When the genuine apostolic fathers were removed from the church, it caused a decline in the apostolic power and function of the church. What was lost is still being restored today!

The Seed of God and Succession of the Kingdom

Spiritual fathering preserves the succession of the kingdom throughout all the generations of the earth. God is a God of succession, mobility, advancement, increase, continuity, and progression. The fathering model secures the succession of the kingdom. God always speak generationally. God never initiates something in the earth for it to be lost to the future generations. Where there’s no proper succession, there’s no advancement, progression, or increase. The whole purpose of reproduction from the beginning was for the seed of God to be passed from generation to the next. One thing you must understand was that Adam was genetically perfect. He was the direct offspring of the father therefore he had no genetic imperfections to inherit. It was the Father’s original intent that the same genetic perfection be passed down to all the generations of the world. This is what the bible calls “the seed of God."

"He that committeth sin is of the devil; for the devil sinneth from the beginning. For this purpose the Son of God was manifested, that he might destroy the works of the devil. Whosoever is born of God doth not commit sin; for his seed remaineth in him: and he cannot sin, because he is born of God. In this the children of God are manifest, and the children of the devil: whosoever doeth not righteousness is not of God, neither he that loveth not his brother" (1 John 3:8-10).

The seed of God is perfect genetics. It's when no sin is found in you. This is the evidence that you have been conformed to the image of Christ. It says, "for his seed remaineth." For something to remain that means abstraction is taking place. Notice at the beginning of the chapter, the context is addressing sonship (matured believer). So when you become a son of God, the chastisement of the Lord is geared towards your perfection. Remember, the chastening of the Lord is in the context of you being a son. God begins to judge the iniquity inside your DNA. This is when the judgements and/or chastisements of the Lord begin to cause an abstraction of the sin nature in you. This is the Father's perfecting process for our maturity when you reach sonship. It's scientifically proven that information and character traits can be inherited or imparted into our genetic makeup. Iniquitous patterns can be inherited in our DNA and through the processing of God these things are abstracted so that the seed of God can remain.

Now this becomes significant when being a son to a spiritual father. God Himself will perfect you, but He also involves your spiritual father in the perfecting process. It was Apostle John addressing his spiritual children in this letter. Many times he referred to them as his "little children." When he said "children", he was measuring their maturity level in the Lord. This is a major function of a spiritual father, specifically an apostolic father. They measure your maturity, they're able to identify what's keeping you from maturing, and they're able to process and equip you to reach the place of maturity.

That's the problem with many in today's church culture, no one wants to be measured and processed to maturity. No one wants to be made anymore! Everyone has a gift and because of the gift they believe their ready for high positions in the kingdom of God. Your gift may open doors, but it's the maturity in your character that will keep you there. Submit to the process! Submit to the governing authority God has placed in your life. You need it for your destiny.

We see that the "call no man father" scripture is not in the context of what many teach. Spiritual fathering is evident all throughout the bible from the old testament to the new. We can refute it! It must be accepted as the will of God and not something to be despised. The problem with today's church is that many of us don't like authority and democracy has brainwashed us into believing we have a choice when it comes to what the Father has clearly laid out in scripture. Let's align ourselves with God's will in this area so that we can get the full benefit of what Jesus died and rose for. There are certain things we cannot access in the kingdom of God without the presence of an earthly spiritual father. Whether you like or agree with it or not, this has been proven so many times.

Chapter 11
Kingdom Faith and the Supernatural

We cannot separate the supernatural from God, nor can we separate the supernatural from the kingdom of God. If the origins of the kingdom are in God who is supernatural in nature, then we can conclude that the kingdom is supernatural too. The process prepares you to legally operate in the supernatural power of God and His kingdom. Far too long preachers have taught and preached the kingdom of God apart from the supernatural. It's easy to read a book, watch Youtube videos, and purchase other materials by our favorite preachers, but can you actually live and demonstrate what you preach or read?

This is why our process is important. It ensures our ability to effectively demonstrate the kingdom we preach about. If we preach the kingdom we should be able to demonstrate all of what comes with it to some degree. In Romans 15:19 the Apostle Paul said, "through mighty signs and wonders, by the power of the Spirit of God; so that from Jerusalem, and round about unto Illyricum, I have fully preached the gospel of Christ." What is the gospel of Christ? It's the gospel that Christ preached which is the gospel of the kingdom.

We can clearly see in the scriptures that the gospel of Christ or the gospel of the Kingdom is confirmed by signs and wonders which are an expression of the supernatural... read Matthew 10. You can do a whole study on this chapter and see the blessings of receiving and responding to the authentic message of the kingdom. You can also see where there are judgements and curses for rejecting the kingdom message and it's messengers. There are persecutions that come with preaching and demonstrating the kingdom message. Lastly, you can see the sacrifices one has to make in order to move in the power and authority of the kingdom. But what I want to point out is verses 5-15. These verses tell us that by preaching an authentic kingdom message, healing, miracles, deliverance (casting out devils), supernatural provision, households (including families) are blessed, and peace is given. When the kingdom of God is present, these things should also accompany it.

The Invisible Reality of the Kingdom

What is the kingdom of God? It's the invisible rule of God in an visible world. So from the realm of the eternal invisible kingdom, wherever the kingdom is present, everything within it's sphere or range has to conform to the standard of the King. Though the kingdom of God is invisible, it's dictates are clearly seen in the visible realm. Whenever Jesus and the apostles announced the good news of the kingdom, sin, demons, sickness, poverty, and even death could not remain. These things cannot live where the kingdom is present. So when you're truly in the kingdom of God, these things should start disappearing in your life.

This is why the process for true kingdom entry is important. "Through faith we understand that the worlds were framed by the word of God, so that things which are seen were not made of things which do appear" (Hebrews 11:3). Even though God and His kingdom is invisible, when it's present, everything naturally has to conform to His standards. Everything that exists now, existed in the kingdom first. Everything that we see now came from the eternal realm of God's kingdom. The kingdom is invisible, but it's not supposed to stay invisible. It's supposed to be seen, felt, experienced, displayed, and demonstrated on a daily basis. According to the kingdom's standard, this is basic Christianity 101. We as a church have majored in the minors and have minored in the majors! What I'm teaching you today is a basic foundation that Jesus laid out for His apostles before they began to perform their early ministry as apostles. What they mastered as disciples qualified them to be trusted as apostles.

Measured by Power

"And I, brethren, when I came to you, came not with excellency of speech or of wisdom, declaring unto you the testimony of God. For I determined not to know any thing among you, save Jesus Christ, and him crucified. And I was with you in weakness, and in fear, and in much trembling. And my speech and my preaching was not with enticing words of man's wisdom, but in demonstration of the Spirit and of power: That your faith should not stand in the wisdom of men, but in the power of God" (1 Corinthians 2:1-5).

First of all, we can see throughout scripture that Paul was a man of revelation, but he was also a man of simplicity. He knew how to articulate the revelatory depths of God's kingdom and he also knew how to articulate the simplicity of it. Even in it's simplicity, the kingdom should come in power. It is a tragedy that American Christianity today is full of preachers who use wise and persuasive words, but demonstrate absolutely no authority or power from God; they are full of the wisdom of this world. This is why many of them can take principles rooted in secularism and carnality, and incorporate it in their teachings. The Apostle Paul was a learned man and understood the value of God's wisdom over the wisdom of this world.

"For this cause have I sent unto you Timotheus, who is my beloved son, and faithful in the Lord, who shall bring you into remembrance of my ways which be in Christ, as I teach every where in every church. Now some are puffed up, as though I would not come to you. But I will come to you shortly, if the Lord will, and will know, not the speech of them which are puffed up, but the power. For the kingdom of God is not in word, but in power. What will ye? shall I come unto you with a rod, or in love, and in the spirit of meekness" (1 Corinthians 4:17-21).

In context, the Apostle Paul was sending his son Timothy (an apostle) to remind the Church of the things that he taught them. Some were arrogant because Paul was supposed to come at a previous time, but couldn't. If the Lord willed, he would come not to just talk, but in power. This is how you handle your critics. Lets look at verse 19 in the Complete Jewish Bible... "But I am coming to you soon, if the Lord wills; and I will take cognizance not of the talk of these arrogant people, but of their power." Paul measured their arrogance with their power level in God and showed them that they didn't measure up.

Some of the most arrogant believers today are ones who are not moving in anything supernatural in God; however, they criticize the ones who are moving in it and accuse them of pride because they refuse to back down to their level of powerlessness. Once you have known the power of God and His kingdom, you don't want to back down and lower your standards ever again! Believe me... I know! "For our gospel came not unto you in word only, but also in power, and in the Holy Ghost, and in much assurance; as ye know what manner of men we were among you for your sake" (1 Thessalonians 1:5).

Importance of Seeking the Kingdom

So how do we move in everything I previously described? That is determined by your hunger level in God and your willingness to submit to His processing for your life. The kingdom is given to those who seek for it. “But rather seek ye the kingdom of God; and all these things shall be added unto you. Fear not, little flock; for it is your Father's good pleasure to give you the kingdom” (Luke 12:31-32).

Seeking denotes something that you need to have and can’t live or function without; it also denotes a pursuit. Proof of desire is pursuit... in order to seek something you have to want it first. It has to be something that you long to find and you won’t rest until you have obtained what you are seeking. When it comes to seeking the kingdom of God and His righteousness, you must have that same drive and determination until you have obtained it. Remember, the kingdom is the invisible rule of God in a visible world. So when it comes to seeking the kingdom, all carnality goes out the door.

I’m amazed at how many can preach “kingdom” and still indulge in the pleasures of the flesh. The kingdom is spiritual in origin so you have to be spiritual and in the spirit to find it. The invisible realm must become your reality. If you’re searching for something of spiritual origin, then you must be like what you’re searching for in order to obtain it. This is why the process is important! It allows iniquity to be removed from your life because iniquity keeps you out of the spirit and bound to the flesh. The kingdom is spiritual first. You must take on the spirituality of the kingdom in which you are seeking so that you won't be deceived by counterfeits during your pursuit.

Dimensions of the Supernatural

Notice that it doesn’t say “seek first God.” Though our goal should be to seek God, it says seek first His kingdom.

There's a protocol to approaching the Father. Most people haven't encountered God directly, they have only encountered extensions of His rule or His kingdom. Just because you're in the kingdom doesn't mean you have direct access to the glory. Remember, the Father sent Jesus to reconcile man back unto Himself. He didn't come Himself, but He sent an extension of who He is, Jesus our high King. Jesus embodies everything the Father is, but He's still not the Father. Just because you've experienced signs and wonders doesn't mean that you're authorized to release signs and wonders. There's a difference between them being released and you being one. Just because you've experienced the glory doesn't mean you're fully authorized to move in that realm. There is a huge difference between experiencing something and operating in it. We go from faith to faith and glory to glory.

There are three dimensions of the supernatural: faith, anointing, and glory. Matthew 6:13 says, "for thine is the kingdom, the power, and the glory." Kingdom, power, and glory corresponds with faith, anointing, and glory. The kingdom realm is a faith realm because you must change your belief and perspective in order to partake of it. The preaching and demonstration of the kingdom will always challenge contrary thought patterns and belief systems. You will never see or move differently until you start believing differently.

Holy Spirit spoke to me while writing this and said, "In order to seek the kingdom, you have to be hungry for alignment" which means, alignment with God's standards, thoughts, ways, heart (which is expressed in what He decrees and are law in the kingdom) etc. Faith gives us sight in the invisible and once our belief system is in alignment with what we see by faith, then we can become a model or a replica of what we beheld in the eternal realm. Faith will enable you to believe the unreasonable and impossible because you no longer walk by natural sight, but spiritual sight. When you live in this reality of the supernatural, you're able to tap into the power of God and do great exploits on behalf of the kingdom of God. The process aligns you with the kingdom as you continue to seek it.

Matthew 6:13 says, "for thine is the kingdom, the power, and the glory; which are three dimensions of the supernatural. Apostle Guillermo Maldonado says something similar in his book, *The Glory of God;* he said the three are faith, anointing, and glory. He also said, "the kingdom is the message of heaven, the power is the ability of heaven, and the glory is the atmosphere of heaven." Jesus demonstrated the message, produced the power, and brought the atmosphere of heaven to the earth; the kingdom realm is the faith realm. It challenges everything you believe and pushes you to the standards of God. You must believe the kingdom message and seek to be in total alignment in every area of your life.

The kingdom is an economic, cultural, and judicial system. Economic deals with the production, development, and management of wealth. Culture deals with ideas, customs, and social behavior of the citizens of the kingdom of God. Judicial deals with the laws of the kingdom, the administration of justice / judgment, the courts of heaven, and the judges of the kingdom. I believe that the judiciary is most important because it governs the other two. The laws of the kingdom of God govern our social behavior and how we receive, handle, and distribute wealth.

People want to move in the power and in the glory realm, but they haven't mastered them. Remember, experiencing the power and glory is different from demonstrating it. Sometimes we get sidetracked by signs and wonders, but that's elementary in the kingdom of God. There are greater realms to experience. Signs, wonders, miracles, healing, and deliverance are major signs of the presence of the kingdom, but we must realize that there are greater demonstrations to be displayed in the earth. I don't just want gold dust, I want gold mountains! The riches in the kingdom are different from the riches in the glory. That's another teaching that deserves greater attention than what I'm able to discuss in this book. It takes matured faith to access all of what the kingdom of God has to offer. But in order for our faith to mature we must first master basic faith.

The Measure of Faith

"For I say, through the grace given unto me, to every man that is among you, not to think of himself more highly than he ought to think; but to think soberly, according as God hath dealt to every man the measure of faith" (Romans 12:3). When you give your life to Jesus, the required measure of faith was imparted into your spirit. This measure is foundational in your walk as a believer. It takes faith to believe in a God you don't initially see. It takes greater faith to remain true to your continual growth in your walk with God. This measure of faith is what I call basic faith that deals with your ordinary daily trust in God. This has nothing to do with believing in big miracles or anything grand. This is basic ordinary faith in the person and ability of God at an entry level. There is nothing wrong with this measure of faith... the problem is when we refuse to graduate from this measure. Man in his own ability and fallen nature does not have the capacity to believe God. This is why divine assistance is needed for us to believe on a greater level. Submission to God's processing for our life will challenge and bring us into greater levels and dimensions of faith.

In context of the scripture above, there were some who became prideful and thought of themselves higher than they should. Apostle Paul addressed the issue by reminding them that the grace and faith they have received is a result of the sovereignty of God, and not by their own limited ability; grounds for boasting in ones ability is taken away. Faith is a divine gift from God and it is Him who enables you to trust in Him. "For by grace are ye saved through faith; and that not of yourselves: it is the gift of God: Not of works, lest any man should boast" (Ephesians 2:8-9). Faith along with grace are gifts from God and cannot be earned in our own ability. We have no right to boast about something that we have not earned or what we need divine assistance in obtaining and executing. It's not by our works! If it was, then we would have the right to boast.

A Gift From God

"Although I was formerly a blasphemer and persecutor and arrogant, but I received mercy, because, not knowing, I acted in unbelief: and the grace of our Lord overflowed with faith and love in the Messiah Y'shua" (1 Timothy 1:13-14 *ONMB*).

Mercy, grace, faith, and love are all gifts from God. The grace of God overflowed to Apostle Paul along with faith and love. These are things to be received as well as given. You don't earn it, it's freely given to you. Paul was rebellious, but he was rebellious out of ignorance. Thank God that He's merciful towards our ignorance! "For unto you it is given in the behalf of Christ, not only to believe on him, but also to suffer for his sake" (Philippians 1:29). It is given unto you to believe on Him and to suffer for His sake. Once again, faith is given not earned. So there is no excuse for our unbelief. Unbelief along with fear are choices that we submit too. When a man is in his flesh, he cannot believe God even for the simplest things. These are things in our heart that God begins to address through the process. So if faith is a free gift, then a gift can either be received or rejected. You can choose to reject it, but know that God has eliminated every excuse for you to walk in fear and doubt. Everyone has the capacity to believe.

The Trying of Your Faith

"My brethren, count it all joy when ye fall into divers temptations; Knowing this, that the trying of your faith worketh patience. But let patience have her perfect work, that ye may be perfect and entire, wanting nothing. If any of you lack wisdom, let him ask of God, that giveth to all men liberally, and upbraideth not; and it shall be given him. But let him ask in faith, nothing wavering. For he that wavereth is like a wave of the sea driven with the wind and tossed. For let not that man think that he shall receive any thing of the Lord. A double minded man is unstable in all his ways" (James 1:2-8).

When you refuse to believe you are unstable. Verse six tells us to ask in faith without wavering. Faith is a choice! Either we receive the faith that's given freely as a gift or we continue on the downward spiral of doubt and fear. When your faith wavers you're unstable. The scriptures say that you are double minded and unstable in all of your ways. Your faith is going to be tried. It's so much easier to the carnal man to doubt and live in fear than to actually believe. When you live in doubt and fear you don't have to contend for anything. In the good fight of faith, you must fight with your faith. The trying of your faith will produce patience. It takes faith to wait on something to happen or manifest that you can't see with your natural eyes. But during that waiting process, God is preparing you for the manifestation.

At the end of verse four, it tells us that we will not want for anything if we allow patience to have its perfect work in us. This begins with the trying of our faith. Your faith will attract opposition. This is why those who are carnal find it easier not to believe and why those who fit in this category find it hard to receive anything from God. The judgements of God also come to try and purify your faith. We will be put in positions to believe God even when He's crushing us; this takes maturity to understand.

"Paul, and Silvanus, and Timotheus, unto the church of the Thessalonians in God our Father and the Lord Jesus Christ: Grace unto you, and peace, from God our Father and the Lord

Jesus Christ. We are bound to thank God always for you, brethren, as it is meet, because that your faith groweth exceedingly, and the charity of every one of you all toward each other aboundeth; So that we ourselves glory in you in the churches of God for your patience and faith in all your persecutions and tribulations that ye endure: Which is a manifest token of the righteous judgment of God, that ye may be counted worthy of the kingdom of God, for which ye also suffer: Seeing it is a righteous thing with God to recompense tribulation to them that trouble you" (2 Thessalonians 1:1-6).

Again, we can see where faith and patience are placed in the same category pertaining to opposition as the result of your faith; your faith will bring opposition and persecution. Part of God's judgements for your life and maturity will come through the trying of your faith. This is not something that we can avoid. In the midst of our opposition we must get to the place where our faith grows exceedingly. The effects of resistance and friction, and through the pain and tightening of our muscles will make us stronger. This is the same effect tribulation and persecution should have on our faith. God allows the trying of our faith and even the pressure from our enemies to make us stronger.

Opposition should make you stronger not weaker. When one becomes weaker that means that they are dominated by fear and doubt. These kinds of people always live in disappointment as it pertains to God in His promises because again, when you're double minded and unstable in what you believe, you won't receive anything from God. Maturity is able to see God even when everything and everyone that's coming at you opposes what God has promised. When Jesus said don't cast your pearls before swine, He followed the same principle.

So what is faith? Faith is when a man or woman's belief system aligns itself with God's reality. Faith is trusting God and doubting the flesh. Faith is conforming your ways and thoughts to God's ways and thoughts. This takes discipline to accomplish. It takes real discipline to have real faith. It is a process of renewing your mind so that genuine transformation can take place. A lot of Christians have a hard time believing God because it requires them to relinquish certain thought patterns. These thought patterns are comfortable to the flesh, but they are contrary to the thought patterns of God. You see, faith is a foundation and all foundations have to be built before it can hold the weight of any structure.

The foundation of faith has to be laid in the heart of an individual and it takes time and processing. We have so many things in us that oppose the kingdom of God. Things that shape our belief system and cause us to live beneath the standard God has set. When you allow the Lord to truly mature you, then your faith will mature too. Until then you will always believe God for low level things and you will always think beneath the standard of God's thought processing. As you mature you graduate from basic faith to dimensional faith.

"Now faith is the substance of things hoped for, the evidence of things not seen. For by it the elders obtained a good report. Through faith we understand that the worlds were framed by the word of God, so that things which are seen were not made of things which do appear. By faith Abel offered unto God a more excellent sacrifice than Cain, by which he obtained witness that he was righteous, God testifying of his gifts: and by it he being dead yet speaketh" (Hebrews 11:1-4).

Dimensional faith allows you to access the reality of the supernatural, pulling it out of the invisible and causing it to materialize naturally. This goes beyond changing natural circumstances or events that already exist. This kind of faith taps into the creativity of God. It causes you to become a creator like your Father in heaven. This kind of faith creates something out of nothing. It exists in heavenly dimensions and pulls it from there causing it to materialize in the earth. The worlds were framed by the word of God. All of this is in the context of faith. You can frame worlds or even your world by your words if your faith is properly aligned with God's reality. This means your reality has to shift. You must come out of the carnal realm and into the God realm. People are too in tuned and in touch with their carnality! In order to operate in the realm where you become a creator, you have to see everything from God's perspective. When you see everything from God's perspective then you will speak from that perspective and you will create like He creates because you are operating from the dimension where He dwells.

Dimensional faith is prophetic in nature. You cannot have this level of faith and not be prophetic. The scriptures say that we prophesy according to the proportion of our faith (read Romans 12:6). Your faith level determines how you prophesy. So if you believe in something erroneously then you will prophesy out of a spirit of error. Prophecy in itself has the power to create; our words had creative ability. Proverbs 18:21 says, "Death and life are in the power of the tongue: and they that love it shall eat the fruit thereof." Power in that verse is the Hebrew word "yad" which means: the power of the hand. It's denoting the creative power behind our words. Out of the abundance of our heart, the mouth will speak (read Luke 6:45).

Whatever your heart is full of will be revealed in your speech. Faith rooted in the heart gives the prophetic word more authority and power to work its way into manifestation. Faith is the engine that mobilizes the vehicle. This is why we must be sure in God and about what He has established so that the manifestation of what we speak will not be canceled out. This is why the process is so important! It challenges our belief systems that are out of alignment with God's reality and we are also challenged to believe from the dimension where God rules.

Ancient Faith

"Jude, the servant of Jesus Christ, and brother of James, to them that are sanctified by God the Father, and preserved in Jesus Christ, and called: Mercy unto you, and peace, and love, be multiplied. Beloved, when I gave all diligence to write unto you of the common salvation, it was needful for me to write unto you, and exhort you that ye should earnestly contend for the faith which was once delivered unto the saints. For there are certain men crept in unawares, who were before of old ordained to this condemnation, ungodly men, turning the grace of our God into lasciviousness, and denying the only Lord God, and our Lord Jesus Christ" (Jude 1:1-4).

According to verse one, these people have already been sanctified. Sanctification or holiness wasn't the issue. In context of the entirety of this book, the problem was the infiltration of false teachers. The saints was instructed to earnestly contend for the faith which was once delivered unto them. "Once delivered" means that they no longer possess it. As it was in those days so it is in our time. A lot of stuff was lost through the dark ages when the Roman Catholics ruled much of the world. Today we find that the Church is centuries behind. This is why God is restoring the ancient revelation, ancient mysteries, and is causing us to dig old or ancient wells. What do I mean by this? Why is it that Moses outranks most apostles today? The glory of the latter is supposed to be greater than that of the former, but honestly we haven't seen the reality of the former in the forefront of our generation.

I had a dream recently that I was in Israel searching for a well. It was a well that was clogged with dirt that I knew I had to dig. The Lord spoke to me as I was reminiscing on that dream and He said, "there are ancient wells of revelation that I gave the people of old that you must dig for your generation to drink from." This took me back to many prophecies that I received in the infancy of my walk stating that I will be like the prophets of old, but now I understand the meaning. The reason is because I (we) must tap into what they had. I'm not saying that we should revert back to the old covenant. I'm saying what the scripture said, "we must earnestly contend for the faith that they had." In that particular passage of scripture, the new covenant was already in effect. So in the new covenant, we cannot just disregard what the saints did in the old. To be honest, there were greater displays of the glory and the acts of God in the old testament than in the new. This is because they tapped into something that we are too carnal to receive.

Contending Faith

We are urged to earnestly contend for the faith that was once delivered to us. When you're earnest about something that means you're serious about it. When you're serious about something, it has grasped your focus. Contend means to struggle or wrestle for control. This also tells us that when you contend for this level of faith, then opposition will come with it. We as believers should be serious about our faith. It's the shield of faith that quenches the fiery darts of the enemy... not your tongues and not your prophecy; prophecy is a weapon of war in your arsenal as stated in 1 Timothy 1:18. Faith will always cause some type of contention with religious antagonists and the works of darkness.

If your faith is not causing some type of contention, then what you call faith is not really faith at all. 1 Timothy 6:12 tells us to fight the good fight of faith. So with faith there is always going to be contention or a battle to obtain whatever that is desired. "I will therefore put you in remembrance, though ye once knew this, how that the Lord, having saved the people out of the land of Egypt, afterward destroyed them that believed not" (Jude 1:5). Unbelief will destroy you and it physically destroyed the saints of old. Nowadays, it can destroy your destiny. Unbelief is a sin and is always causing you to fall short of the glory of God. Romans 14:3 teaches us that "anything outside of faith is sin." ALL sin is a result of some type of unbelief.

Only Believe

"...Be not afraid, only believe" (Mark 5:36). Fear is proof that unbelief is present. Fear is also a sin because it's not of faith. Fear of trusting God, fear of the opinions and disapproval of man, fear of rejection, fear of making a mistake, fear of missing it, fear of being wrong, fear of walking in pride, fear of deception, fear of the unknown, and unhealthy fear of God are all things that prove you are an unbeliever. God doesn't sympathize with your fear. Anything that's outside of faith, I admonish you to get rid of it! Anyone who would question or challenge your faith, remove them from your proximity or circle immediately. "These signs shall follow them that believe", so if you truly believe then signs should follow you.

The signs that follow those who don't believe are: they won't be able to cast out devils, their speech will always be carnal and full of earthly sensual wisdom, they will live in constant fear of what might not happen if they do step out there and decide to trust God, they will never have enough faith to heal the sick, they will always remain on the outer courts of the kingdom of God, they will always remain powerless, they will stay sick, they will stay broke, they will continue to bust their behinds for what God always gives for free, and they always submit themselves to what seems impossible. They will always be "there" but not "in."

Just like Jesus did in Mark 5:40, you have to put all unbelievers or things that might encourage you not to believe out of your proximity. These people and things don't need to be close to you. That's how earnest you need to be about your faith. In Genesis 15:6, Romans 4:3, Galatians 3:6, and James 2:23 it tells us that Abraham believed God and because he believed God, it made him righteous. Faith makes you righteous before God. Why? Because faith will always be proved by your obedience to God. Faith without works is dead

(read James 2:17). Even when you read Hebrews 11, you will see that faith and obedience was always correspondent with one another. In James 2:23, it shows us that this is how Abraham became a friend of God. In John 15:14 Jesus said, “you are my friends if you do what I command." Friendship is another level of intimacy with God that most believers have not obtained.

Friends share secrets and friends become vulnerable to one another because the bond of trust is strong. God loves everybody, but He doesn’t trust everybody. God’s trust in you has to be proven through your trust in Him which is proven by obedience to His commandments in faith.

Pursuit Of Him In Faith

True faith will cause you to pursue God. Read Hebrews 11:6... Do you see how faith is followed by diligently seeking God in this scripture? Your faith is also proven in how diligently you seek God. These are simple keys to seeing the supernatural demonstrated in your life. “And he said, Hear now my words: If there be a prophet among you, I the Lord will make myself known unto him in a vision, and will speak unto him in a dream. My servant Moses is not so, who is faithful in all mine house. With him will I speak mouth to mouth, even apparently, and not in dark speeches; and the similitude of the Lord shall he behold: wherefore then were ye not afraid to speak against my servant Moses" (Numbers 12:6-8).

Moses was faithful or full of faith. The Complete Jewish Bible says that Moses was the only one who was faithful in His house. So Moses was the only one full of faith and willing to go the distance with God. Wow! Your diligence and faithfulness determines your positioning in God. Moses had what the others didn't have because he was faithful; he was willing to pay the price to see God face to face. Moses wasn't perfect and made mistakes, but he was faithful. He had a passion for the glory of God. That's why he experienced it and was able to demonstrate it before the people. The stuff that the saints of old walked in makes our stuff look pathetic! We must dig that well of faith that those men of God had. Their obedience to God was absolute and without question. Yes... many of them weren't perfect (some of them were), but they had a passion for God that drove them to center their entire existence around what God wanted and they dismissed any desire of the flesh. This is the faith that God is looking for.

People who say they love God must get back to passionate pursuit of not just His presence, but also His person. There are many who call Him Father, but they don't know Him as Father. There are many who call Him friend, but they are not known by Him as friend. There are many who call Him master, but they don't know Him as master. The Father loves everyone, but He doesn't relate to everyone the same way. We sing worship songs full of names and terms we call Him, but we are not truly close enough to intimately relate to Him in the way we're singing to Him.

Many get caught up in a "moment" of worship, but they don't live a life of worship. A moment in His presence is not equivalent to being immersed in a habitation of His presence and getting to know Him as a person. When you come to God you must believe that He is. "He" denotes the fact that He's a person. He not a mist, gold dust, gemstone, or any of that. These things can accompany Him, but they are not who He is. We must desire to know Him above all and it takes genuine faith to pursue Him in this manner. This is why God was with Moses and Abraham and why He called them friends.

Chapter 12
Dethroning the Spirit of Mammon in Your Life

"Lay not up for yourselves treasures upon earth, where moth and rust doth corrupt, and where thieves break through and steal: But lay up for yourselves treasures in heaven, where neither moth nor rust doth corrupt, and where thieves do not break through nor steal: For where your treasure is, there will your heart be also. The light of the body is the eye: if therefore thine eye be single, thy whole body shall be full of light. But if thine eye be evil, thy whole body shall be full of darkness. If therefore the light that is in thee be darkness, how great is that darkness! No man can serve two masters: for either he will hate the one, and love the other; or else he will hold to the one, and despise the other.

Ye cannot serve God and mammon. Therefore I say unto you, Take no thought for your life, what ye shall eat, or what ye shall drink; nor yet for your body, what ye shall put on. Is not the life more than meat, and the body than raiment? Behold the fowls of the air: for they sow not, neither do they reap, nor gather into barns; yet your heavenly Father feedeth them. Are ye not much better than they? Which of you by taking thought can add one cubit unto his stature? And why take ye thought for raiment? Consider the lilies of the field, how they grow; they toil not, neither do they spin: And yet I say unto you, That even Solomon in all his glory was not arrayed like one of these. Wherefore, if God so clothe the grass of the field, which to day is, and to morrow is cast into the oven, shall he not much more clothe you, O ye of little faith? Therefore take no thought, saying, What shall we eat? or, What shall we drink? or, Wherewithal shall we be clothed? (For after all these things do the Gentiles seek:) for your heavenly Father knoweth that ye have need of all these things. But seek ye first the kingdom of God, and his righteousness; and all these things shall be added unto you. Take therefore no thought for the morrow: for the morrow shall take thought for the things of itself. Sufficient unto the day is the evil thereof" (Matthew 6:19-34).

Changing Your Value System

Verses 19-20: "Lay not up for yourselves treasures upon earth, where moth and rust doth corrupt, and where thieves break through and steal: But lay up for yourselves treasures in heaven, where neither moth nor rust doth corrupt, and where thieves do not break through nor steal."

In this passage of scripture, Jesus was teaching His disciples to change their value system. In order to properly understand and become partakers of the kingdom, we must change our value system. What we value will reveal who is our true master. Jesus was teaching the disciples not to value the treasures on earth. He clearly stated that the treasures of earth were corruptible and were able to be stolen. When you place your value in earthly treasures you will end up losing. By Jesus commanded His disciples to lay up treasures in heaven, He was teaching them to value heavenly things above earthly things. This is key in obtaining earthly wealth God's way.

Verse 21 says, "For where your treasure is, there will your heart be also." What you value, you will put your heart into. If you value earthly treasures, then your heart will go into obtaining earthly treasures. If you value the treasures of heaven, then your heart will go into obtaining heavenly treasures. We have been trained through the fall of Adam and Eve to value earthly treasures above heavenly treasures. When man was in the garden, his only labor was maintaining what was produced out of the presence of God. Adam didn't have to work hard! He mainly had a job of maintenance instead of hard labor. It was his rebellion that caused him to work by the sweat of his brow to survive. When he was in the garden with his wife, it was not so. We've been taught to value things that are earth bound. Because of the fall, Adam had to depend on the earth to survive instead of depending on God to live. Jesus was refocusing His disciples and shifting their minds back to the original blueprint. True prosperity comes from an intimate relationship with God, not busting your butt for a little of nothing!

Verse 22-23 says, "The light of the body is the eye: if therefore thine eye be single, thy whole body shall be full of light. But if thine eye be evil, thy whole body shall be full of darkness. If therefore the light that is in thee be darkness, how great is that darkness!" Jesus was teaching His disciples to focus solely upon kingdom treasures. "Eye" in this passage denotes your focus. What you focus on, you will become. Jesus was telling them to get single focused on the things of the kingdom and not the things that are earth bound only. Proverbs 23:7 says, "as he thinketh in his heart, so is he."

When your heart and focus is in alignment with the treasures of heaven, what has captivated your focus will begin to fill you in becoming the treasure of the kingdom. "But we have this treasure in earthen vessels, that the excellency of the power may be of God, and not of us" (2 Corinthians 4:7). When you become full of what has your focus, then your entire life begins to not only come into alignment with it, but you start producing the fruit of what has been planted in your spirit. In the Jewish bible, to have a single (good) eye is equivalent to being generous, and having an evil eye is equivalent to being stingy. Verse 24 says, "No man can serve two masters: for either he will hate the one, and love the other; or else he will hold to the one, and despise the other. Ye cannot serve God and mammon." "Mammon" in Greek is the word "mammonas" and it means: wealth, treasure, riches, and confidence. What is the revelation? One who is under the dominion of the spirit of mammon, is one who puts his confidence in his riches. Mammon is not money; it is the prince that rules over the love and corruption of money. The Bible calls mammon a master. Master in this passage is the word "kyrios" and it means: to whom a person belongs, master, and Lord.

It originated from the word "kuros" which means supremacy. When you're under the dominion of your paycheck, then you're bound by mammon. When you're defined by how much money you have and don't have, then you're bound by mammon. When you're subject to earthly currencies in any way, then you're under the rulership of this spirit. Money is supposed to work for us, not us work for it. In the beginning, Adam's increase worked for him, but after the fall he worked for increase. He became subject to what was once subject to him. Jesus was clear when He said that you cannot be mastered by God and mammon at the same time; only one of these would be in charge.

The Origins of Mammon

Mammon originated from the Syrian god of riches which came from Babylon. In order to understand mammon, we must understand it's origins. In the scriptures, we see the origins of Babylon when the tower of Babel was built. These people attempted to erect a structure that would reach all the way to heaven. This happened under the rule of Nimrod who became a very powerful ruler during his time. It was because of this that he became even more prideful, overseeing the erection of this tower to reach heaven so that he could claim equality with God. Because of their pride and wealth during that time, the Babylonians thought they became independent from God. They became so self confident, prideful, and arrogant that they thought they could build their own way to God to dethrone Him from His place of sovereignty.

This is what happens with many of those who become very wealthy. They start valuing their wealth over the God who gave it to them. This causes pride to eventually have one to resist the authority of the Father in their life. When financial prosperity has gone to ones head, they start acting like they have brought their life back from the Father to run it their own way. This is why the Bible says that you cannot serve God and mammon. Mammon will literally cause you to resist God. It gives you false power over your own life to choose the path that God has not ordained for you. Mammon is a spirit that rests on money and it controls you through money.

It tells you to overspend or to spend unnecessarily in an attempt to keep up with the Jones'! It tells you to be stingy and to look out for yourself only and that you cannot do the will of God because you don't have enough money. It tells you what you can and cannot have. Anything that will have a negative effect on your life and ministry as the result of the presence of or the lack of money, is the result of the presence of mammon. Mammon will keep you bound to the world's economy and totally ignorant to the economy of the kingdom of God. This is why Jesus told His disciples not to place their value in earthly treasures.

Wisdom and Wealth

Proverbs 16:16 says, "How much better is it to get wisdom than gold! and to get understanding rather to be chosen than silver!" "Wisdom" in Hebrew is the word "chokmah" and it's defined as: skill in war, wisdom in administration (process of running a business, management, activities that relates to running an organization), shrewdness (having or showing an ability to understand things and make good judgements, sharp intelligence), prudence (careful good judgement that allows someone to avoid danger or risks) in religious affairs.

Wisdom teaches you how to fight smart and not hard. There are too many believers trying to bind the devil with no results. The reason why believers fight so hard and lose so much is because of the lack of wisdom when it comes to the spirit realm and spiritual affairs. Wisdom is not just knowing, but it's “knowing how." Even the gifting of the word of wisdom deals with the application of directives or instructions based upon what has already been revealed. Wisdom gives us strategy in war so we'll know what to do based upon our knowledge of our authority, covenant rights, and the devices of our enemies. This means that wisdom also deals with spiritual legal matters in the life of the believer.

Wisdom is the ability to apply knowledge based upon understanding, and knowing when and how to apply it. It helps you to discern the timing of God concerning certain matters that you would like to move forward in. Wisdom is the ability to apply knowledge and revelation. When one is wise, he is skilled in making sound decisions and judgement calls concerning certain matters. Our decisions determine our wealth. Everyone is currently where they are in life as the result of their decisions. Decisions are made based upon priority. So what you deem most important or give a place of priority in your life will affect your decision making, which will draw the outcome of your overall financial status. If I can change your priorities, I can change what you believe. If I can change what you believe, I can change your choices. If I can change your choices, I can change your status. This is how wisdom can be applied to improve your life.

When you begin to live by the wisdom of God, it is the result of your understanding. When you truly understand something, you have comprehended it, and have began to govern your life by it. Understanding is the prerequisite for application. To understand means "to stand under" and goes beyond basic knowledge. You can know something and still not submit or govern your life by it. Knowledge is when you have obtained information. Understanding is when the information has obtained you; this is when you begin to govern your life by the information that you have received. Your wisdom level is demonstrated in your application of the knowledge which has obtained you.

When you learn to value wisdom over money, then money will come as the result and mammon still won't have a foothold in your life. When God asked Solomon in a dream what he desired, Solomon asked for wisdom to govern the people. God said, "because you didn't ask for great wealth or even victory over your adversaries, I will give you wealth." When you govern your life by the principles of God, wealth will come. Proverbs 4:7 says, "Wisdom is the principal thing; therefore get wisdom: and with all thy getting get understanding." Wisdom deals with the application of principles. Once you have understanding, then wisdom can be applied. When you value wisdom, you value the way God operates. His ways of operation always seem strange to the carnal man. 1 Corinthians 3:19 says, "For the wisdom of this world is foolishness with God. For it is written, He taketh the wise in their own craftiness." If the wisdom of this world is foolishness with God, then the wisdom of God is foolishness with man. What God calls wisdom will be foolish to those who are carnal.

Test of Giving

Acts 2:45 and 4:34-35 demonstrate how generosity in giving keeps you from under the dominion of mammon. Giving to leaders, the work of God, the saints, and the poor will ensure that you're not under the dominion of mammon. Giving was one of the first things the early church was tested in. When the community was being formed, immediately giving of possessions was included in their foundational customs and practices. I would say that if you're stingy, then you're not in the kingdom of God. The early church in their infancy stage saw great amounts of growth and conversions because they were selfless and everything they did was for the benefit of the whole community. Could you imagine what our local assemblies would be like if we all were that selfless about our leaders and fellow brothers and sisters in Christ?! No one would be in debt or would lack anything. The church is it's own answer to debt and lack within its own local community. Until we get from under the dominion of mammon and stop withholding from God and our local assembly, we will never see debt totally eradicated from the Church. The strategy is right there in the scriptures!

God Wants Your Heart

First thing we need to understand is that God is not after your money, He's after your heart. Because your heart is in what you treasure (your money), that's the first thing God will go after. Matthew 6:21 says, "for where your treasure is, there will your heart be also." God is interested in what grips your heart. "And when he was gone forth into the way, there came one running, and kneeled to him, and asked him, Good Master, what shall I do that I may inherit eternal life? And Jesus said unto him, Why callest thou me good? there is none good but one, that is, God. Thou knowest the commandments, Do not commit adultery, Do not kill, Do not steal, Do not bear false witness, Defraud not, Honour thy father and mother. And he answered and said unto him, Master, all these have I observed from my youth. Then Jesus beholding him loved him, and said unto him, One thing thou lackest: go thy way, sell whatsoever thou hast, and give to the poor, and thou shalt have treasure in heaven: and come, take up the cross, and follow me.

And he was sad at that saying, and went away grieved: for he had great possessions. And Jesus looked round about, and saith unto his disciples, How hardly shall they that have riches enter into the kingdom of God! And the disciples were astonished at his words. But Jesus answereth again, and saith unto them, Children, how hard is it for them that trust in riches to enter into the kingdom of God! It is easier for a camel to go through the eye of a needle, than for a rich man to enter into the kingdom of God. And they were astonished out of measure, saying among themselves, Who then can be saved? And Jesus looking upon them saith, With men it is impossible, but not with God: for with God all things are possible. Then Peter began to say unto him, Lo, we have left all, and have followed thee. And Jesus answered and said, Verily I say unto you, There is no man that hath left house, or brethren, or sisters, or father, or mother, or wife, or children, or lands, for my sake, and the gospel's, But he shall receive an hundredfold now in this time, houses, and brethren, and sisters, and mothers, and children, and lands, with persecutions; and in the world to come eternal life. But many that are first shall be last; and the last first" (Mark 10:17-31).

Morals will not get you into the kingdom. This rich young ruler was a man with morals, but he was also a stingy man. This is a good example of how the love of money will grip your heart to make you forsake God to keep your worldly status. Why is it so hard for rich people to enter into the kingdom? It's because when you already "have it all", you don't feel like you have to depend on God for anything. Again, this is why the process is so important! It teaches you how to depend on God and His system for results. The process humbles you and causes you to forsake your way for God's way. People tend to function independently from God when they have everything that they need. Who needs faith when you have everything you need? This is a very dangerous attitude.

If you have heard the testimonies of men of God who have obtained great wealth, you'll also hear how God either had to strip them or how they started off with nothing before they became wealthy. We clearly see that whatever we give up for the sake of Christ and the kingdom, God plans to restore a hundredfold in this lifetime. God does not have an issue with wealth. The issue comes when wealth has gripped our heart and we operate independently from God. Before God will give you wealth, He has to teach you how to trust Him and work the principles for financial increase so that you can possess wealth the kingdom way.

Fear of Loss

Fear of loss keeps many out of the kingdom of God. Matthew 10:34-39 says, “Think not that I am come to send peace on earth: I came not to send peace, but a sword. For I am come to set a man at variance against his father, and the daughter against her mother, and the daughter in law against her mother in law. And a man's foes shall be they of his own household. He that loveth father or mother more than me is not worthy of me: and he that loveth son or daughter more than me is not worthy of me. And he that taketh not his cross, and followeth after me, is not worthy of me. He that findeth his life shall lose it: and he that loseth his life for my sake shall find it.”

We see that in the kingdom of God you must lose your current life to gain your real life. Sometimes increase in God and from God will only come where there is loss. The counterfeit must make way for the authentic. Wealth gained in corruption must be removed to make way for the wealth that will be gained by being in covenant with God. We must understand that wealth can be gained apart from God but that is what makes it corruptible. This is why we must store up our treasures in the kingdom or in heavenly places, so that out of our relationship with God we can extract (by faith and obedience) the resources of the kingdom. Hear me in the Spirit!

Seeking the Kingdom and His Righteousness

Fear of loss is a huge sign that mammon has dominion in a person’s life. Matthew 6:25 says, “Therefore I say unto you, Take no thought for your life, what ye shall eat, or what ye shall drink; nor yet for your body, what ye shall put on. Is not the life more than meat, and the body than raiment?" "Take no thought" does not mean don't handle your personal business in properly stewarding your financial affairs. It means don't live in the fear of never having enough. The presence of the kingdom destroys lack. This is why the Bible says to seek first the kingdom of God and His righteousness, and your necessities will be added to you. "Righteousness" in Matthew 6:33 is defined as justice or virtue which gives each man his due. The root word of that in the Greek is "díkaios" and it's defined as observing divine laws.

Seeking first the kingdom deals with you submitting your life to God and His kingdom, and conforming your life to the ways of the kingdom by applying it's principles daily. Only carnal minded people seek their needs. Fear causes you to see your need bigger than the supply of the kingdom. You must learn to live in the supply of the kingdom. This only happens when you allow your life to be conformed to it's standard. You must learn to consistently apply God's principles so that you can live in constant supply of the kingdom. In seeking the kingdom of God you are seeking to be submitted, committed, and conformed to God's laws of operation. Seeking the kingdom has everything to do with aligning your life with His laws and standards.

Wicked Stewarding and Dishonest Gain

Read Luke 16:1-13. This parable describes a wicked steward whose fraud had been discovered by his lord. The wicked steward realizes that he's about to get fired and put out on the streets, so he cleverly goes to all the people that owes his boss money. He discharged certain debts owed to his lord after accepting payments from them that were substantially less than the actual amounts owed. This "favor" was given so that when the steward was fired and put out on the streets, the ones he showed favor to would show favor to him by letting him stay in their home. It was in this context that verse 9 comes into play: "Now what I say to you is this: use worldly wealth to make friends for yourselves, so that when it gives out, you may be welcomed into the eternal home." Jesus was being sarcastic in this verse, not literal. Dishonest gain and mishandling of funds may gain you friendships with the wrong people, but Jesus guarantees failure if wealth is gained in this manner. Jesus has no problem with wealth. It only becomes a problem when it's gained dishonestly or outside of covenant with God.

In verse 8, it talks about the children of this world being wiser than the children of light. In context it's speaking of the shrewdness in the dishonesty of the unjust steward as it pertains to how he possessed his wealth. This man had strategy when it came to his evilness. There are divine strategies that God wants to give the saints so that we can possess wealth the kingdom way. We must rid ourselves of all dishonesty regarding how we handle our money and how we respond to God with our money.

When you put God first financially, He will sanctify and increase you. When the early church was established, giving was one of the first things that they mastered. Read Acts 2:42-47 and Acts 4:32-37. The unity of the saints in conjunction with their submission to the apostles and their doctrine produced a supernatural environment. Signs, wonders, numerical growth, and financial increase was the portion of the early church because they were submitted to the apostles, their doctrine, and they were unified with one another. Most blame the leader for the failure of a church, but that thought is not entirely accurate e.g. Moses and Israel in the desert. Submission and unity literally erased poverty from the early church. No one was broke because everyone was generous.

Speaking of being generous, let's talk about how they gave in the New Testament. Giving and wise stewardship will break the back of poverty in your life and it will bring you from under the dominion of mammon; mammon subjects you to the world's system.

According to the scriptures, church funds were for:

1. Apostolic Leadership - 1 Corinthians 9:1-14 CJB. "Am I not a free man? Am I not an emissary of the Messiah? Haven't I seen Yeshua our Lord? And aren't you yourselves the result of my work for the Lord? Even if to others I am not an emissary, at least I am to you; for you are living proof that I am the Lord's emissary. That is my defense when people put me under examination. Don't we have the right to be given food and drink? Don't we have the right to take along with us a believing wife, as do the other emissaries, also the Lord's brothers and Kefa? Or are Bar-Nabba and I the only ones required to go on working for our living? Did you ever hear of a soldier paying his own expenses? or of a farmer planting a vineyard without eating its grapes? Who shepherds a flock without drinking some of the milk? What I am saying is not based merely on human authority, because the Torah says the same thing — for in the Torah of Moshe it is written, "You are not to put a muzzle on an ox when it is treading out the grain."[a] If God is concerned about cattle, all the more does he say this for our sakes. Yes, it was written for us, meaning that he who plows and he who threshes should work expecting to get a share of the crop. If we haves own spiritual seed among you, is it too much if we reap a material harvest from you? If others are sharing in this right to be supported by you, don't we have a greater claim to it? But we don't make use of this right. Rather, we put up with all kinds of things so as not to impede in any way the Good News about the Messiah. Don't you know that those who work in the Temple get their food from the Temple, and those who serve at the altar get a share of the sacrifices offered there? In the same way, the Lord directed that those who proclaim the Good News should get their living from the Good News".

Most of the time when the Apostle Paul addressed the area of giving (especially to leadership) it was because of the church's stinginess. They would allow other apostles to make merchandise of them, but when it came to their own apostolic father, he received scraps or nothing at all. This is why Apostle Paul decided to work with his own hands many times, but we know that it was not God's original intent. There is a demand on senior leadership (particularly apostolic ministry) and it adds greater stress upon the leader when they have to lead people and work hard too. In the beginning of Acts 6, the church continued to grow and the Gentiles began to complain because the Hebrews were getting better treatment in the meeting of daily needs. They complained to the apostles, but the apostles told the people that we cannot stop and wait tables, they have to be solely devoted to prayer and ministry of the word. This is why seven people were appointed to serve in that capacity. That's how great of a demand it is on senior leadership!

In 1 Timothy 5:17-18, "Let the elders that rule well be counted worthy of double honour, especially they who labour in the word and doctrine. For the scripture saith, thou shalt not muzzle the ox that treadeth out the corn. And, The labourer is worthy of his reward". We can see that double honor is in the context of giving to leadership. You cannot say that you truly honor your leadership and never put any money in their hands or have not given anything of value to them. When you don't give to leadership you're showing double dishonor. It shows that you don't value your impartation. Giving to leadership is one of the major ways to see supernatural provision in your life. This is seen in Philippians 4:10-19 with Paul and it is also seen in 1 Kings 17:7-16 with Elijah and the widow woman. When you meet the needs of the man of God, God will meet your needs.

2. Believers In Need - Acts 2: 44-45 "And all that believed were together, and had all things common; And sold their possessions and goods, and parted them to all men, as every man had need". Acts 4:32-37 "And the multitude of them that believed were of one heart and of one soul: neither said any of them that ought of the things which he possessed was his own;

but they had all things common. And with great power gave the apostles witness of the resurrection of the Lord Jesus: and great grace was upon them all. Neither was there any among them that lacked: for as many as were possessors of lands or houses sold them, and brought the prices of the things that were sold, And laid them down at the apostles' feet: and distribution was made unto every man according as he had need. And Joses, who by the apostles was surnamed Barnabas, (which is, being interpreted, The son of consolation,) a Levite, and of the country of Cyprus, Having land, sold it, and brought the money, and laid it at the apostles' feet".

1 Corinthians 16: 1-4 CJB "Now, in regard to the collection being made for God's people: you are to do the same as I directed the congregations in Galatia to do. Every week, on Motza'ei-Shabbat, each of you should set some money aside, according to his resources, and save it up; so that when I come I won't have to do fundraising. And when I arrive, I will give letters of introduction to the people you have approved, and I will send them to carry your gift to Yerushalayim. If it seems appropriate that I go too, they will go along with me".

3. Widows Who Had No Other Family To Rely On - 1 Timothy 5: 3-16 CJB "Show respect to widows who are really in need. But if a widow has children or grandchildren, first let them learn to do their religious duty to their own family and thus repay some of the debt they owe their forebears, for this is what is acceptable in the sight of God. Now the widow who is really in need, the one who has been left all alone, has set her hope on God and continues in petitions and prayers night and day. But the one who is self-indulgent is already dead, even though she lives. And instruct them about this, so that they will not be open to blame. Moreover, anyone who does not provide for his own people, especially for his family, has disowned the faith and is worse than an unbeliever. Let a widow be enrolled on the list of widows only if she is more than sixty years old, was faithful to her husband, and is known for her good deeds — as

one who has reared her children well, showed hospitality, washed the feet of God's people, helped those in trouble, and engaged in all kinds of good work.

But refuse to enroll younger widows, for when they begin to feel natural passions that alienate them from the Messiah, they want to get married. This brings them under condemnation for having set aside the trust they had at first. Besides that, they learn to be idle, going around from house to house; and not only idle, but gossips and busybodies, saying things they shouldn't. Therefore, I would rather the young widows get married, have children and take charge of their homes, so as to give the opposition no occasion for slandering us. For already some have turned astray to follow the Adversary. If any believing woman has relatives who are widows, she should provide relief for them — the congregation shouldn't be burdened, so that it may help the widows who are really in need".These were the main reasons for the collection of funds in the early church, but notice that I did not mention the tithe. The tithe was agricultural (read Leviticus 27:30-32). According to Numbers 18: 21-24, the tithe compensated the Levites and the Levites were required to tithe unto the priest. Read Numbers 18:25-29.

New Testament giving is free will giving, cheerful, and at times sacrificial giving. There are no limits on New Testament giving. Giving ensures that you're not bound by the spirit of mammon and that there's no limit as to what you're willing to give that's of value to the Father. This doesn't mean that the church is supposed to pay all of your bills. If you properly steward your own financial affairs then you should be able to pay your bills. Church funds are supposed to be for those in leadership and those who are in need.

Chapter 13
Pride: Your Exit Out of the Kingdom

Pride is the mother of all sin. It was the first offense and royal sin against the Lord. This is how Lucifer lost his place in the kingdom of God. This is why submitting to God's process and desiring His judgements in your life is the most important thing you could ever do. So what is pride? Pride is a high or inordinate opinion of one's own dignity, importance, merit, or superiority. Pride is not thinking highly of yourself or having high self esteem about yourself -- it is excessively thinking too highly of yourself. Pride is when we see ourselves beyond the measure that God has set. In order to properly examine your measure you must understand God's value system. You must realize that there will always be someone greater than you. It's hard for prideful people to submit properly. They always see themselves as higher or more than everyone they meet. When you think of yourself too highly than you should, it is hard for you to submit to others in the correct measure that you are supposed to.

Pride and Honor

Prideful people can never honor correctly. Scripture tells us to give honor to whom it is due (read Romans 13:7). Everyone is not due the same measure of honor. This is even established in the Godhead. The Father is due the highest measure of honor. Jesus does not even take the glory and honor due to the Father for Himself like Lucifer tried to do. The Holy Spirit always reveals Jesus to us and also the Father.

speaks nothing of Himself (read John 16:13). If there is submission and honor in the Godhead then what makes us so different? The chief of police doesn't have the same measure of authority and honor the mayor has. The secretary of state has a measure of honor due, but the president of the United States has a greater measure of honor due. People who are overly proud have a hard time submitting to and properly honoring someone else especially if that measure of honor is greater than what they have received.

In 1 Samuel 24, we can recall where David was fleeing from Saul. David begin to live in the wilderness of Ein-Gedi and word had gotten back to Saul about where David fled to. Shortly after his arrival, Saul encountered a cave in which David and his men were hidden. Not knowing David and his men hid themselves in the cave, Saul entered to cover his feet and use the restroom. Now this was a moment where David's character was being tested. David's men kept trying to push David to slay Saul. It was the perfect moment to take vengeance on the man who caused him to be in that situation. Instead of slaying Saul, David decides to cut off a piece of his robe. David did this because of the constant pressure from his men to slay Saul. However, David had enough conviction to know that Saul was still the Lord's anointed and that's someone that you do not touch even if he is wrong.

This was the perfect opportunity for David to flex his muscles and to a degree he did by cutting the edge of Saul's robe. At that moment, David still had a little pride that manifested. Pride is manifested when given an opportunity or platform to exude itself. What David did was show that he could kill Saul, but chose not to. This is pride in action. David didn't want to sin by touching the Lord's anointed, but he didn't want to look weak in front of his men either and his ego got the best of him. This was why God allowed him to be run off into the wilderness in the first place. The wilderness process exposes all of your hidden iniquities and pride, and to show that he was wrong for cutting a piece of Saul's robe. 1 Samuel 24:5 states that David's heart smote him because he cut a piece of Saul's robe. He realized that he dishonored the Lord's anointed by trying to prove a point to his men. This is what most Christians refuse to understand. Whether a leader is right or wrong, it's not your place to correct, reprimand, or dishonor them. Only those who are or have gone through a true process understand this.

Honor is something that has been lost to the body of Christ for quite some time now. David immediately recognized his pride and quickly humbled himself. Then he corrected his men for wanting him to kill Saul. What's amazing to me is that David still saw himself as a son and a servant of Saul. Even after all that Saul did to him, he was still submitted in his heart to Saul. David still called Saul his master (in verse 6), his lord (in verse 10), and his father (in verse 11). David still honored Saul even in his wrong. Most Christians think that it is okay to rebel or break covenant with God ordained leadership because they are wrong. We can clearly see here that this was not the way God dealt with David. You cannot change who your spiritual father or mother is. Just like you cannot change it naturally, you also cannot change it in the spirit. Saul was David's father in the kingdom regardless of his wrong.

David defeated pride within himself and humbled himself before his father. Though he wasn't necessarily under his father's rule anymore, he still had to honor that rule. David still had to honor the government his father carried even though it was used to persecute him. Regardless of Saul's wrong, as king there was still a certain measure of honor due to him. Anything less than that would be a violation of God's universal principle of honor. Believers who desire to remain immature will not receive this.

In Job 41, there is a demonic creature that God rhetorically questions Job about. This creature's name is Leviathan. Through God's questioning we can see the major characteristics of those who is under the influence of this spirit. Job 41:34 calls him the king of all the children of pride. So when it comes to pride in any individual, it is actually an issue of lordship. This is why the Lord resists the proud so much, especially those who say they are believers. It is an issue of lordship. We cannot be mastered by two masters. Just like Mammon is a master, Leviathan is a master too. We cannot have pride and call Jesus our Lord. This is why God is so hard on pride. When we accept the grace of God in our lives, that is our opportunity to allow the Lord to rid any and all pride out of our lives.

Pride is embedded in basic human nature. It is the fallen nature we have inherited from Adam. It is something that we all must overcome. As I will show you a little later on, no one can conquer this within themselves by themselves. Only God can conquer this and it has to be crushed out of you. There are so many people in the body of Christ right now who are living off of the fumes of grace and have not properly submitted themselves to the Lordship of Jesus because they refuse to allow Him to process them to crush all pride within them. This is why so many Christians never reach the height of their destiny and is also why we lack in so many areas. We can't expect to receive the full benefits of a kingdom that we are not fully a part of. Leviathan is a chief ruler in the kingdom of darkness. He is a king in that realm.

A piece of him is in all of humanity and in order to fully enter the kingdom of God, we have to allow God to conquer this within us at all cost! It's just that serious! Let us look at some of the questions God asked Job about Leviathan. That way we can accurately identify the presence and operation of this spiritual king. Some verses I will skip over because they coincide with other verses and subjects that will already be mentioned.

You Can't Cast Out Leviathan

Job 41:1-2 says, "Canst thou draw out leviathan with an hook? or his tongue with a cord which thou lettest down? Canst thou put an hook into his nose? or bore his jaw through with a thorn?" It is impossible to dethrone Leviathan's power and influence in a person's life. Your gifts, anointing, or authority doesn't have the capability to dethrone this spirit. It takes the Lord Himself to accomplish this. You cannot even address Leviathan's rank or power without the Lord being with you in a special way and granting you His full empowerment to do so. No human power or supernatural anointing can cause Leviathan to lose his post. Now, an individual can decide to humble themselves and come out of agreement with this spirit, but it takes God to break its grip off of an individual. Those who are possessed by him can also operate under the anointing. There are prideful people who operate under the anointing and are prideful because of the gift of grace given to them. Many don't realize that God doesn't wait until you are perfect to anoint you. He anoints you in your imperfection. It's not by your works, it's by His grace and election. Pride cannot be cast out. Pride must be processed out of your character in order for leviathan to lose its grip on your life.

Prayerlessness and Harsh Speech

Job 41:3 says, "Will he make many supplications unto thee? will he speak soft words unto thee?" Those who are prideful have weak prayer lives. Supplications are one of the manifestations of prayer. The position of prayer is always a position of humility. Supplication is made to one who is higher in authority. Prideful people have a hard time positioning themselves in any position of humility to person or power higher than themselves. This spirit is also the spirit that hinders prayer movements and consistent prayer in the lives of believers.

Leviathan hates prayer! This spirit seeks to convince those under its control that they have what they need and they do not need to ask God or anyone else for help. Pride prevents people from asking and this is why many do not receive. Also those who are proud will not speak soft words. People who are unfriendly or abrasive in their speech all the time are ruled by Leviathan. It's hard for these kind of people to have any lasting friendships. Pride destroys good friendships and the tongue is used in the destruction of these friendships. People who are unkind, unloving, rude, harsh, and condemning in their speech are full of pride. It's time to get on that potters wheel and let God make us over again!

Covenant Breakers And Entitlement Complexes

Job 41:4 says, "Will he make a covenant with thee? wilt thou take him for a servant for ever?" Those who are ruled by Leviathan are serious habitual covenant breakers. It's hard for them to keep any real friends. Eventually all of the friendships they forge will be broken. These people exemplify unfaithfulness. They cannot commit to anything that's covenant such as marriage, spiritual parenting, mentoring, friendships, or employment. This is also foundational for the forming of a vagabond as well. Those who wander from place to place, job to job, marriage to marriage, house to house, church to church, spiritual father to spiritual father are those who are covenant breakers.

Because of this, they become wanderers who never really fully commit in their heart to anything or anyone. They are too independent to make a covenant with anyone. Those who are highly independent are ruled by Leviathan. They feel as though they need no one and will see to it that no one will have any kind of say in their life. There is no longevity with covenant breakers. These people even break covenant with God. All of this is the fruit of pride which puts one under the rulership of Leviathan. This spirit is known to break up marriages, friendships, and other covenant relationships. Also, Leviathan keeps the ones under his lordship from benefiting from any kind of covenant. The Bible is a book of covenants. This spirit keeps many out of the promises of God because God's promises are based on the covenant He has made with us.

Those who are under the lordship of Leviathan also have an attitude of entitlement. Instead of serving until God decides it is time for elevation, these people will come in already expecting a position. This may be as a result of "how long" they have been in ministry or the fact that they are tired of waiting on God. People who are power hungry or eager for positions of authority are ruled by Leviathan. These people will even serve for a while, but their motive isn't pure. "Wilt thou take him for a servant for ever?" They won't serve long! If their expectations are not met then eventually they will come to you and tell you that their "season" is up. Those who can't serve long are bound by pride and Leviathan.

Even when it comes to employment, you have to watch those people who can't keep a job long. This is why regardless of their title in their previous ministry, when people want to come under our oversight and discipleship locally, one of the first things we test is their ability to serve. If you can't serve people then you can't serve God. Pride will not serve or will not serve long. Pride always want to be on top. Pride wants everyone else to submit without them being submitted. These are destructive behaviors that can only be dealt with by submitting to the processing of God for our life and destiny.

Destructive And Cannot be Tamed

Job 41:5 says, "Wilt thou play with him as with a bird? or wilt thou bind him for thy maidens?" Leviathan is not a creature to take lightly or to play with. You cannot bind Leviathan in a person's life and it cannot be controlled. Pride cannot be tamed and causes destruction. Proverbs 16:18 says, "Pride goeth before destruction, and an haughty spirit before a fall." Pride always precedes destruction. Destructive people are prideful people. I have been around people who destroyed everything they touched. Come to find out, these people have very strong traits of pride in their life. It never fails! The destruction in the lives of these people and through the life of these people cannot be contained. Ones who are bound by pride must submit to God's processing for their life so that Leviathan can no longer have legal ground to cause destruction in their own lives and the lives of others they come in contact with. Until then, these people will always leave a path of destruction everywhere they go.

Job 41:8 tells us that if we try to battle Leviathan on our own, then we will remember the battle and do it no more. Again, this spirit cannot be tamed! I don't care how much apostolic rank and authority you have, you cannot tame or control Leviathan. Leviathan gains his legal ground because of the condition of ones heart. You can rebuke Leviathan and cause his operations to cease for a time, but to cast him out or control him, you cannot do. This takes the Lord's doing and the person who is bound must submit to the Lord's processing.

Resist The Spirit of God

Job 41:15-17 says, "His scales are his pride, shut up together as with a close seal. One is so near to another, that no air can come between them. They are joined one to another, they stick together, that they cannot be sundered." Leviathan's pride is in his scales. His scales are so tightly sealed together that no air can get in. The spirit or the Holy Spirit is always represented by air according to the Greek and Hebrew. So Leviathan prides himself on his ability to resist the Spirit of God. Those who cannot flow in the gifts of the Holy Spirit are under the rulership of Leviathan or they are battling it. Those who cannot discern the movement of the Spirit, are less sensitive to the Spirit, and have a hard time feeling His presence are under Leviathan.

Leviathan is also protected and defended by his scales. Prideful people are always defensive. This is why it is so hard for prideful people to get delivered. There are other spirits that protect Leviathan from attack. These are the representation of his scales. Leviathan works with other spirits such as rejection, lust, hurt, fear, self righteousness, intimidation, insecurity, shame, and religious spirits. These spirits are normally encountered while ministering deliverance to those who are bound by pride. In order to destroy Leviathan's hold on an individual, all these other scales (spirits) must be addressed. Leviathan's scales must be stripped.

A Tongue Of Fire

Job 41:19 says, "Out of his mouth go burning lamps, and sparks of fire leap out." Let's look at another reference to fire. Remember it says out of his mouth goes the burning lamps and sparks of fire. In James 3:5 it says, "Even so the tongue is a little member, and boasteth great things. Behold, how great a matter a little fire kindleth!" The tongue is a little member, but boasts great things. Boasting is another manifestation of pride. To boast means to speak with exaggeration or excessive pride, especially about oneself. Leviathan also manifests through other verbal manifestations like lying, gossip, cursing, as well as boasting.

Those who cannot control their tongue are dominated by Leviathan. Those who don't know how to properly or honorably talk to people, those who are always short, snappy, and harsh in their speech, and those who are quick to get angry and curse people out etc., are all bound by Leviathan. Pride always manifests by way of speech. If it's in the heart then it will come out of the mouth. Leviathan always destroys with his mouth. Gossip, slander, backbiting are all included in this. So those who cannot control their tongue are under the lordship of Leviathan.

Easily Angered And Cause Strife

"Out of his nostrils goeth smoke, as out of a seething pot or caldron" (Job 41:20). To "seethe" means: to foam as something is boiling and to get violently excited or agitated. Those who are easily agitated have a strong root of pride in their heart. This scripture is a reference to anger. Those who are easily angered have pride. Anger is usually a manifestation of pride. This seething pot can also represent stirring up strife. Proverbs 28:25 says, "He that is of a proud heart stirreth up strife…." Those who are easily given to strife and conflict and are easily angered by them are bound by Leviathan. Those who are easily angered cannot get along with other people and they always have a "justified" reason why. Pride always seeks to justify contention and strife.

Stubborn And Rejoice at the Misfortunes of Other

"In his neck remaineth strength, and sorrow is turned into joy before him" (Job 41:22). Leviathan's strength is in his neck. A strong neck refers to being stiff-necked or stubborn. Those who are stubborn also manifest rebellion. Those who are stubborn are ones who refuse to change and are stuck in their ways. This is also pride and manifests with leaders a lot. Many of them refuse to change the pattern and structure of their ministry to accommodate what the Spirit of God wants to do with their ministry. They remain stuck in the same old pattern with no change and no growth. Churches who don't operate in the gifts of the Holy Spirit fit this category. There are ministries who resist any kind of change outside of their place of comfort.

Even older people who are stuck in their ways manifest this stubbornness. It's all under the lordship of Leviathan. Many feel because they are older they have seen it all and know it all. This is what I call the pride of age. You may have seen a lot and you may know a lot, but you do not know it all nor have you seen it all. Do I believe seniors should be honored? Yes I do. I also believe that no one, regardless of their age, should be so stuck on what was and what they believe that they can't change. Some people are so stuck that they will never change anything. This is all pride! Stubborn people resist change. Even when God attempts to bring change, they are resistant to it. This is dangerous! Don't let that be you.

Prideful people also rejoice when others sorrow and rejoice at the misfortunes of others. They take pleasure in the misery of others. This is not the love of God. I don't care if these people hurt you or have betrayed you. You should never rejoice at their misfortune. Jesus didn't rejoice over the death of Judas. So why are we rejoicing when our enemies fall? I know people right now who pray that their natural (human) enemies be destroyed. That is witchcraft! Jesus, Peter, and Paul only released the judgement of God on certain individuals as the Spirit of God permitted them too. They were never loose with their mouths when it came to curses and judgements like some of us are. Then you have to understand that the authority they walked in during their time on the earth, no one else walked in. Not even the other apostles had the same measure of authority these men had while they were on the earth. We are never to rejoice when others fall, no matter what they have done to us. We can be relieved without rejoicing.

Hardened Heart

"His heart is as firm as a stone; yea, as hard as a piece of the nether millstone" (Job 41:24). When your heart is hardened you cannot receive love or correction. I used to be like that. I can remember a place in my life where my emotions were so dull and cold. I went through a lot of emotional and mental turmoil during my adolescent years. Many people that I love and trusted hurt me. So to prevent myself from getting hurt again, I became cold, uncompassionate, and uncaring about people. I was the one to give my last until I became cold and callous towards people. I manifested my pride to protect me from being hurt or disappointed again. On the inside I deeply wanted to love people, but I couldn't. At least not until I surrendered my life to the Lord and allowed Him to judge these things within my heart and character. I didn't get free until I allowed the Lord to chip away all of the stony pieces around my heart to give me a new heart of love, compassion, forgiveness and mercy towards other people. Those who struggle with love, compassion, forgiveness, and showing mercy are those whose hearts are hardened. This can't be cast out, this has to be dealt with over time and processing.

Intimidation and Control

"When he raiseth up himself, the mighty are afraid: by reason of breakings they purify themselves" (Job 41:25). When Leviathan is stirred he tries to strike fear into even the strongest of people. Those who are prideful can be very intimidating. To intimidate means: to frighten some to get them to do what you want them to do, to force into or deter from some type of action by inducing fear. Intimidation is always for the purpose of control. Those who are intimidating are also very controlling. Controllers always use fear to enforce compliance. This is also another manifestation of witchcraft. This is all under the lordship of Leviathan.

Leviathan Will Always Be Exposed

"I will not conceal his parts, nor his power, nor his comely proportion" (Job 41:12). Though Leviathan is a demonic king in Satan's kingdom, God is dedicated to exposing his operations in the earth. There is nowhere where Leviathan operates where God won't expose him. This is why pride is so evident and it cannot be hidden no matter how much you try to hide it. Pride will always manifest openly. This is an eternal law. Lucifer tried to keep his operations a secret, but the iniquity of pride in his heart eventually manifested openly for all of heaven to see. No matter how much you try, you cannot hide pride. I have seen people who act humble in front of people while inwardly their heart is full of pride. Even in pretending to be humble you can see the pride and arrogance in how they talk, walk, and interact with people. False humility is still a manifestation of pride. You cannot hide it. God is dedicated to exposing all of Leviathan's operations.

No One Can Conquer Leviathan

"The sword of him that layeth at him cannot hold: the spear, the dart, nor the habergeon. He esteemeth iron as straw, and brass as rotten wood. The arrow cannot make him flee: slingstones are turned with him into stubble. Darts are counted as stubble: he laugheth at the shaking of a spear. Sharp stones are under him: he spreadeth sharp pointed things upon the mire" (Job 41: 26-30). No weapon of war can defeat Leviathan. Not a spear, a dart, a sword, a slingshot, tongues, prophecy, spiritual warfare, or such things alike. Much of the questions asked in Job 41 shows man's inability to conquer Leviathan. Pride is such a deeply rooted iniquity and spirit that it takes God Himself to defeat this thing within man. No man can match Leviathan's strength and power. It takes the authority of Jehovah to defeat it. Verse 33 says, "Upon earth there is not his like, who is made without fear." There is no demonic entity like this in all of the earth. This is one of Satan's top generals and is a king in Satan's kingdom. There are not many demonic spirits that are referred to as kings in the bible. This should tell you something about him.

Humility is the antidote to pride. Though we cannot conquer Leviathan in our own power and strength what we can do is choose to humble ourselves. Fasting is one way to do that. Psalm 35:13 tells us that fasting humbles the soul (mind, will, emotions, and intellect). So through fasting we weaken Leviathan's power over our life, but it's the Lord that destroys Leviathan's power in our lives altogether. This is only accomplished through the process of the Lord.

Celestial Pride

Celestial pride is when your pride or arrogance is rooted in your spirituality or spiritual position. Spiritually gifted people with no true process are a danger to the body of Christ on so many levels. We see this all throughout the church of Corinth. They were a spiritually gifted church, but they were full of all kinds of immorality and pride. They challenged Paul who was their apostolic father on a few occasions. They even challenged his apostolic authority and Paul found himself defending his apostleship to those who were under his measure of rule and authority in the Church. This is because spirituality without governance breeds rebellion and witchcraft. It is my belief that the more spiritually gifted or anointed you are, the more submitted and governed you must be. Those who claim to be spiritual or anointed, but despise government, their spirituality is not real and their anointing is tainted. King Nebuchadnezzar is a classic example of celestial pride.

Though he also had terrestrial pride in his earthly possessions and position as king, he also had a "God complex" which caused him to erect a statue of himself for others to worship. He was to be the sole focus of worship. We cannot allow our spiritual gifts and positions to corrupt us. Those who are not truly broken and humbled by God are a major danger to the body of Christ. You need this process! You need to learn the humility and meekness of Jesus Christ. Jesus has the second highest rank and position in the entire universe next to the Father. You see Him walking in such authority, but you never see Him abusing His power or letting His power get to His head. Jesus was always humble to the Father.

Pride and Offense

Another major manifestation of pride during your process is offense. Offense is one of the most deadly traps the enemy uses to get people to forfeit their destiny. Offense is how the Pharisees and most of the rest of the Israelite nation missed the kingdom of God. Jesus came and brought what they were looking for, but because they allowed offense to set in they missed their time for visitation. Their offense was prophesied in the book of Isaiah 8:14-15 which says, “And he shall be for a sanctuary; but for a stone of stumbling and for a rock of offence to both the houses of Israel, for a gin and for a snare to the inhabitants of Jerusalem. And many among them shall stumble, and fall, and be broken, and be snared, and be taken.”

See how a stone of offense and a rock of stumbling go together in this passage? Let's look at Romans 9:30-33: “What shall we say then? That the Gentiles, which followed not after righteousness, have attained to righteousness, even the righteousness which is of faith. But Israel, which followed after the law of righteousness, hath not attained to the law of righteousness. Wherefore? Because they sought it not by faith, but as it were by the works of the law. For they stumbled at that stumblingstone; As it is written, Behold, I lay in Sion a stumbling stone and rock of offence: and whosoever believeth on him shall not be ashamed.”

One of the reasons why the Gentiles attained righteousness is because they didn’t get offended by the Gospel. Israel with all of their “righteousness” or their perception of it, still did not attain righteousness because of offense. It’s hard for offended people to see what’s good for them. Offended people never obtain the promises of God because they allow offense to harden their heart to what's being presented because it's not according to their personal traditions or feelings. Israel was more concerned with their being right instead of righteous. Most people don't realize that you can be "right" and not be righteous. Israel kept the traditions and the law of Moses faithfully, but they became unrighteous because they were offended at Jesus. Offense will bring you out of right standing with God. All of your works of doing right means nothing if you have an easily offendable heart. Offense will cause you to reject the good that God brings because it challenges you and shows you that you're not where you think you are. Offended people have a false sense of righteousness. They believe their being "right" (in their own eyes) justifies their rebellion. This is wrong.

What is Offense?

Before we go any further, what exactly is offense? Offense comes from the Greek word "skandalon" which is defined as: a snare, a noose, a trap, an impediment placed in the way and causing one to stumble, any person or thing by which one is entrapped. Offense is a snare or entrapment designed to cause one to stumble or impede their progress. While preparing this the Lord spoke to me and said, "resentment is the root of offense." Resentment is defined as bitter indignation at having been treated unfairly. So when one feels wronged by another, if it's not handled immediately within the heart of the individual that was wronged, then resentment takes root and springs forth into offense. Offenses come through people.

Luke 17:1 says, "Then said he unto the disciples, It is impossible but that offences will come: but woe unto him, through whom they come!" The only way to avoid offense is to avoid people and that's not realistic. You can't stop people from committing offenses against you, but you can prevent yourself from becoming offended by choosing to forgive quickly.

The word scandal comes from the Greek word "skandalon". Scandal is defined as a rumor or malicious gossip about events or actions, disgraceful events or nasty gossip about the private lives of others. This type of offense comes based upon the negativity you hear about another person. This is why I never go by what's said about an individual when I meet them. I would rather discern or see it for myself if something negative is there, than to let someone poison my heart about a person before I actually get to know them. Offended people are always around or involved in gossip.

You have to watch those people who always "know something" or "heard something" about people. If someone is always bringing it to them, you need to watch that too. Offended people are magnets for slander and gossip. They're loyalty cannot be trusted. An offended person is always easily offended by a person they don't like or a person who does something that easily offends them. This makes it easier for them to put their mouth on such people. The actual offense makes one feel that they are justified to slander or spread gossip about a person. This is wicked.

Offenses will always come through the words of people. James 3:2 says, "For in many things we offend all. If any man offend not in word, the same is a perfect man, and able also to bridle the whole body." So we know that offenses will come and they will mainly come through the words of people; however if we master not being offended and master not offending with our words, at that point is when we will become perfected. We cannot help how people choose to receive stuff, but we can help how we deliver it. The gospel itself offended the religious people of Jesus' day because these people already had resentment towards Jesus; He was the Messiah.

God Uses Offense to Try Your Heart

God will use offense to try your heart. He will use offense to expose your motives, your love for God, and your willingness or unwillingness to obey God. The Pharisees put on an outward act of holiness and righteousness, but when Jesus came on the scene their offense quickly exposed their wickedness. The scriptures tell us that God tries the heart.

"I the Lord search the heart, I try the reins, even to give every man according to his ways, and according to the fruit of his doings" (Jeremiah 17:10).

"Oh let the wickedness of the wicked come to an end; but establish the just: for the righteous God trieth the hearts and reins" (Psalm 7:9).

"The fining pot is for silver, and the furnace for gold: but the Lord trieth the hearts" (Proverbs 17:3).

The word "trieth" in Hebrew is the word "bachan" (baw-khan) and it means: to examine, to prove, to test, and to scrutinize. It is biblically proven that God tries your heart to prove it. God tries your heart to expose where you are with relationship and in your maturity with Him. He will even use things like slander and gossip to try your heart so you can see where you are. Your reactions to these things show your maturity level and it reveals whether or not you are easily offendable. Isaiah 48:10 says, "Behold, I have refined thee, but not with silver; I have chosen thee in the furnace of affliction." In the Complete Jewish Bible it says: "Look, I have refined you, but not [as severely] as silver; [rather] I have tested you in the furnace of affliction." God uses affliction to test you and to prove where you are with Him. How you handle your testing and proving will determine whether or not you will be elected or chosen by God. He proves who He chooses. So many people get offended at the affliction that they become blind to anything that God is doing in midst of it. Offense blinds you to the fact that God is proving and preparing you for destiny.

1 Peter 2:8 (CJB) says, "also he is a stone that will make people stumble, a rock over which they will trip. They are stumbling at the Word, disobeying it — as had been planned." The King James Version will also confirm that the word is a rock of offense, a stumbling stone that Israel stumbled over causing them to disobey it. Offended people stumble at the word, they can't obey it. Their hearts are so consumed with offense that they are blinded to the processing of God in their offense. Then in the Complete Jewish Bible it says "as had been planned" at the conclusion of the above passage. God plans according to your offense.

You want to know why things are not going right in your life? Check your offense level. You don't want to be like ancient Israel where God has to give what you are supposed to have to another person because you couldn't endure the afflictions and the tryings of the Lord. If you are easily offendable then believe me when I tell you this, God has a replacement for you in case you refuse to relinquish your offense. God always has a "Plan B" for offended people. I don't know about you, but I do not want God to have a "Plan B" for me!

The Foundation of a Traitor

Those who are easily offended will betray you no matter how long they have been with you. You have to watch those people who cannot stand when adversity comes. Adversity is another method God uses to test and prove you. I don't trust people who crack every time something hard comes. This tells me that the right amount of pressure will cause you to leave me hanging or to betray me. You have to be careful not to trust those with weak faith and little to no endurance when hardship hits them.

I'm not saying don't love them and treat them mean, I'm saying not to invest your confidence in their their loyalty towards you. True loyalty is tested in the furnace of longevity. I don't trust anyone who can't go through the fire with me or who can't stand with me in my greatest moments of persecution or failure. People who can't stand in the midst of adversity will turn on you no matter how long they have been with you. “And then shall many be offended, and shall betray one another, and shall hate one another” (Matthew 24:10). Being offended goes into the same category as being one who betrays and one who hates.

Those who are offended will betray you and hate you regardless of what status of relationship you had with them prior to the offense being exposed. The scriptures say that “many shall be offended." Offense is more common than we realize. We must address this issue head on or else we will continue the legacy of raising a bunch of disloyal rebellious vagabonds who run at the first hint of adversity and hardship. Proverbs 24:10 says, “If thou faint in the day of adversity, thy strength is small.” Offended people are weak people. We are urged to be strong in the Lord, not weak in the faith.

Offended People Will Betray God Ordained Leadership

Offended people are always unstable. They don't submit to leadership long especially when they feel like the leadership is wrong about something. These very same people will even try to use holiness and righteousness to dishonor authority. God will never tell you something or show you something that will undermine authority. Offended people will quickly turn into vagabonds and they will become fugitives of accountability. Offended people are always on the offensive. If a leader corrects them about something they may be embarrassed about, in their own defense they may go on the offense and become insubordinate and defiant. When an offended person feels wronged by someone, especially authority figures they become very defiant. When they are in this state of mind and heart, it's hard to reason with these people and give them any wise counsel. These type of people cannot stay committed to covenant relationships long whether it be with spouses, God ordained leadership, friends, or family.

I know that everyone goes through times of transition. Some people have legitimate reasons for removing themselves from under a leader. I have been a victim of abuse of spiritual authority myself. I understand the emotional and mental abuse this causes. I also understand what it means to be restored from this as well. But I have met people who have been to three different churches in three years. I've also met people who have switched from five different spiritual parents within a three year time period. These people claimed to have "legitimate" reasons for leaving from under those whom "God said" was their spiritual father and mother. Anyone who goes through these kinds of patterns have a root of offense in their heart. If you can't keep any lasting relationships with any of your spiritual leaders and you always have "legitimate" excuses as to why you left then the problem is not them, it's you! Your offense is turning you into a vagabond and vagabonds have no authority in the kingdom. Just ask the seven sons of Sceva (read Acts 19)!

In the kingdom of God, true loyalty is forever. There is no time limit on loyalty. Watch those people who do this... "I've been with you for fifteen years pastor." There's no time limit to loyalty! I wasn't always loyal myself. God had to teach it to me. I can remember when my previous leader put me out of the church quite a few times for things I didn't even do. She was wrong for how she treated me, but her wrong didn't cause me to become disloyal. I stood on what God said when He sent me there. The Lord ended up speaking to the woman of God and told her to bring me back in. Around that time I didn't know the

Lord was teaching me the things I'm relaying to you right now. He used affliction and trials to try my heart. I was very faithful to my leader regardless of the wrong she did towards me. Today in the American church what I described to you would be grounds for many to stay away, become bitter, and slander their previous leader. God showed me that wasn't His way. Jesus teaches us to be kind to those who do us wrong regardless of who they are and how much they hurt us.

Now I'm really getting ready to ruffle some feathers with this next statement... There's no where in scripture that justifies leaving from under leadership because they have mistreated you. A lot of times what we perceive as mistreatment is really offense because we didn't like what our leader said. I'm not saying that we should commit to anyone that wants to harm us on purpose, but I'm just stating biblical facts. 1 Peter 2:18 says, "Servants, be subject to your masters with all fear; not only to the good and gentle, but also to the froward." Harsh treatment is not a legitimate excuse to break covenant with leadership. David endured harsh treatment from Saul until his physical life was in danger. In most cases where people are offended by leadership I don't see anyone's physical life being in danger, sexual harassment, or abuse. I just see people who are offended by something they don't like or agree with. Even when David had to flee from Saul, he still called Saul his father, his master, and the Lord's anointed. Offended people lose honor and respect for leaders that they feel have wronged them. This is unbiblical and wicked in the eyes of the Lord.

Fast forward to David's reign as king, he had a son named Absalom who rebelled against him because he nursed offense in his heart over a period of time. Absalom had a sister named Tamar and a brother named Amnon who was sexually interested in his sister. Amnon liked her to the extent that he faked a sickness and convinced his father David to send Tamar to bring him food. When Tamar arrived, Amnon raped her. When Absalom found out he didn't say anything good or bad, but he hated his brother for what he did to their sister. Just because no one says anything doesn't mean that offense is not there. Two years later Absalom plotted to kill his brother. What started as an offense turned into hatred and then murder. Amnon was definitely wrong, but Absalom should have sorted this issue out with his brother instead of letting hatred build up to the place where he would deceitfully plot to murder his brother. Offended people cannot be trusted. They will secretly hold stuff in their heart against you and plot on you because they have developed a hatred for you. Offense always turns into hatred.

This is how you biblically handle offense that may try to develop in you... "Put on therefore, as the elect of God, holy and beloved, bowels of mercies, kindness, humbleness of mind, meekness, longsuffering; Forbearing one another, and forgiving one another, if any man have a quarrel against any: even as Christ forgave you, so also do ye. And above all these things put on charity, which is the bond of perfectness" (Colossians 3:12-14). Most Christians fail at this and is also why they never mature. Charity (love) is the bond of perfection. If you want to be perfect, then master walking in love no matter what. When offenses come, choose to love and forgive. I'm not saying you have to trust, especially when one is proven untrustworthy, but everyone deserves a chance to be forgiven, loved, and restored. David could have allowed offense to set in, but instead he kept his heart in God and the Lord vindicated him in the end. Offense prevents God from vindicating you even if you are the one who was wronged. Offended people always seek to vindicate themselves and to prove that they are right. This will prevent you from becoming a traitor. Offended People Will Believe for a While Then Turn Away Because of Hardship and Persecution

"And these are they likewise which are sown on stony ground; who, when they have heard the word, immediately receive it with gladness; And have no root in themselves, and so endure but for a time: afterward, when affliction or persecution ariseth for the word's sake, immediately they are offended" (Mark 4:16,17). "They on the rock are they, which, when they hear, receive the word with joy; and these have no root, which for a while believe, and in time of temptation fall away" (Luke 8:13).

Most offended people have a soft side to them. This is how others get deceived by the hardness of their heart. The softer side of them is what causes them to receive the word with joy and gladness initially and is also the part of them that deceives people. This is why I'm not impressed by those who have the appearance of humility and gratefulness. Those who have a stony heart are those who are easily and quickly offended according to the parable of the sower. These people will receive the word with joy in the beginning until they are faced with affliction, persecution, and temptation. Because they are not rooted, they are able to believe the word for a while until temptation comes and they fall away. So according to the two scriptures mentioned above, those who have stony hearts will immediately get offended when affliction, persecution, and temptation comes because of the word. Let's accurately define these three words so we can get a better understanding of how and why offense comes.

Affliction - The Greek word for affliction is "thlipsis" (thlip-sis) and is defined as: a pressing, a pressure, and tribulation. The root word for thlipsis is the word "thlibo" (thlee-bo) which means: to press as grapes, to press hard upon, and to squeeze. This deals with the Godly pressure to produce the oil and new wine upon your life. When you receive a word from God, He will test your capacity to handle the weight of that word.

This is not demonic opposition or warfare, this is the pressure of God deflating your pride and preparing you to host the word you received. He does this by squeezing everything out of your life by applying pressure to you. If you get offended during this time you will miss God in that particular season of your life. He may use various things to squeeze you like rebuke, chastisement, serving in hard positions, sitting you under leaders who are hard on you, etc. This also involves the discipline of the Lord preparing you for full sonship. If you cannot recognize God in your process, then you already failed. It's important to see the working of God in you during hard times of pressure and processing.

Persecution - This word comes from the Greek word "diogmos" (dee-ogue-mos), which is from the root word "dioko" (dee-o-ko) and means: to make to run or flee, put to flight, drive away, to pursue in hostile manner, to harass, to trouble, and to molest. This deals with the warfare the enemy brings against you as the result of the word that you received. This may involve the enemy directly or him using other people to drive you away from the promises of God. Most of our persecution comes from agents of the enemy (via people), but it's not limited to spiritual attacks on the mind and body.

Offended people will break down after constant persecution. Most persecution comes from people and when people feel as though they are losing a grip on you, they will do whatever it takes to drive you back into the place you were. Don't let offense because of persecution drive you back to the place where God has brought you from. Stand your ground and believe God!

Temptation - This word in the Greek is the word "peirasmos" (pi-ras-mos) which means: a trial or a proving. It comes from the root word "peirázō" (pi-rad-zo) which means: to try and to test for the purpose of ascertaining quality.

Remember, the scriptures declare that the Lord will try your heart. He will arrange things to happen in your life to prove you so that you can see where you are. Deuteronomy 8:2 says, "And thou shalt remember all the way which the Lord thy God led thee these forty years in the wilderness, to humble thee, and to prove thee, to know what was in thine heart, whether thou wouldest keep his commandments, or no." God will use the wilderness to prove you. Many don't like God's methods, but they are effective. This is different from the chastening of the Lord. This is done to prove your heart towards God and what He has established. It's not for the purpose of discipline, it's for the purpose of exposure. Sometimes only humiliation can produce humility because some people are too blinded by their own pride to humble themselves.

Basic Signs Of Offense

Withdrawal From Relationship - Offended people shut out everyone and can't keep any lasting friendships, relationships, or covenants.

Distrust - Offended people lose trust for everyone.

Unanswered Prayer - When one holds on to offenses, the unforgiveness that comes along with it will keep your prayers from being answered.

Rebellion - Offended people will go against established order. They will use their offense to justify their rebellion. This is wicked!

Recollection of Events - Offended people have a good memory about the things that offends them. If you committed an act of offense against them, believe me when I tell you that they remember it and in great detail!

Unforgiveness - It's hard for offended people to forgive. They feel like they have the right not to forgive a person. When you don't forgive, then God can't forgive you.

This is why we must forgive quickly and love unconditionally. We must pray for our enemies and confront issues biblically. We must not give any foothold to the enemy in our hearts. "And the servant of the Lord must not strive; but be gentle unto all men, apt to teach, patient, In meekness instructing those that oppose themselves; if God peradventure will give them repentance to the acknowledging of the truth; And that they may recover themselves out of the snare of the devil, who are taken captive by him at his will" (2 Timothy 2: 23-26).

It's hard for offended people to remain gentle and patient. Have you ever encountered someone who's always hard? What we can pull from this scripture is that offended people are always involved in strife. They're not gentle, but impatient and unrepentant. Remember, offense is a snare or a trap. Verse 26 speaks to the snare of the devil which is offense. Offended people are always involved in strife. Again, these people are not gentle, they are impatient, and they are unrepentant. Anyone with these characteristics are people who are easily offended and are caught in the snare of devil. Those who are offended don't give instruction in meekness like the scriptures command. They are very harsh and brash teachers. They teach from a place of offense and they go on the offensive while teaching. I'm not talking about preaching from a place of boldness either. People who always preach about how people hurt them or left them are offended. It's time that healing and deliverance come to some of these preachers so that they won't spew that contamination across the pulpit. It's hard for offended people to repent. Because they feel as though they are "right" about how they feel, they see no need to repent. This is how many are deceived by offense.

Revenge?

"Dearly beloved, avenge not yourselves, but rather give place unto wrath: for it is written, Vengeance is mine; I will repay, saith the Lord" (Romans 12:19). We are commanded not to avenge ourselves. "Avenge" in Greek is the word "ekdikeo" (ek-dik-eh-o) which means: to vindicate one's right, to protect and defend one person from another, and to punish a person for a thing. We are commanded not to defend ourselves, vindicate ourselves, or to punish those who do us wrong. It's not our job! We are to place those who do us wrong in the hands of the Lord. Let me also establish this: You can address someone's wrongdoing towards you without being vengeful in your heart and wanting them to be punished for what they have done. Look at how God deals with us. He doesn't fully punish us for all the crimes we have committed against heaven so we shouldn't want to do that to others. If we treat people how God treats us, then we won't fall short in this area. If you belong to God then He will avenge the wrong done towards you. You will be tested in this area and I hope you pass.

Ministry Offense

Most ministry offense is when people are offended by truth or processing from their leader. Many people don't like to hear things like "you're wrong", "you're not ready", "that wasn't anointed", "you missed God on that one", or "that's not God speaking to you." We must get to the place where we desire truth even if it hurts our feelings. It is the truth that will make us free. Our love for the truth keeps us from falling prey to the lie. The Holy Spirit is also called the Spirit of Truth (read John 14:17; 15:26). You cannot say you have the Holy Ghost and not love the truth!

"Even him, whose coming is after the working of Satan with all power and signs and lying wonders, And with all deceivableness of unrighteousness in them that perish; because they received not the love of the truth, that they might be saved. And for this cause God shall send them strong delusion, that they should believe a lie: That they all might be damned who believed not the truth, but had pleasure in unrighteousness" (2 Thessalonians 2:9-12).

If you do not have a love for the truth, many things can happen: you are open to be deceived by lying signs and wonders; more susceptible to come under a false anointing; easily deceived by false apostles and prophets; easy to manipulate to the place where you come under someone else's false anointing, who will ultimately pimp your gift. Your unrighteousness deceives you into thinking that you are righteous because you have rejected the truth and chosen to believe a lie. This is a judgement from the Lord!The scriptures say that when you don't love truth, God sends you a strong delusion so that you should believe the lie.

When the truth offends you and you do not accept it, you become deceived in your unrighteousness. When you're unrighteous that means that you are no longer in right standing with God, His principles, or His order. Unrighteousness means that you have now stepped out of alignment and have submitted to a false anointing and a false order. The scriptures say you are damned when you are in this state. Verse 12 in the passage above talks about the pleasures of unrighteousness. Did you know that unrighteousness is pleasurable? It makes you feel good. It makes you feel like you are right because you feel "peace" about it. So many people are led by a false peace and a false witness in their spirit. Unrighteousness makes you feel good because things appear to be going right after you have stepped outside of alignment. Unrighteousness also makes you think because you have signs and wonders that you are speaking the truth. We should never become that arrogant that we are fooled into thinking such a thing. Some folks better read Matthew 7!

Offense in ministry comes when people hear specific truths that they don't want to hear. It also comes when a certain vessel speaks truth to you whom you don't think isn't qualified to speak to you let alone the truth they bring to you. "Then came his disciples, and said unto him, Knowest thou that the Pharisees were offended, after they heard this saying? But he answered and said, Every plant, which my heavenly Father hath not planted, shall be rooted up. Let them alone: they be blind leaders of the blind. And if the blind lead the blind, both shall fall into the ditch" (Matthew 15:12-14).

Offended people will always be uprooted and are never planted a.k.a. church hoppers!They will never be planted long anywhere. Leaders: you don't ever have to feel bad when people leave your ministry or covering. I'm talking about the leaders who are truly doing the will of God. Jesus said that every plant His Father has not planted will be uprooted. God doesn't plant offended people. You have to be positioned in order to be planted by God. God may send you to a place, but He doesn't truly allow you to be planted until you rid yourself of offense and submit yourself to truth. Those who don't love truth will always live in offense. The Pharisees were offended by what Jesus said because they refuse to accept truth. Therefore God sent them a strong delusion that they may believe the lie. What truth has God previously tried to present to you that you rejected? You many want to revisit that to make sure there is not curse on your life. When was the last time a particular teaching offended you? When was the last time a man or woman of God said something or done something that offended you? Truth that offends you is truth that you will stumble over. You stumble at the rejection of it; truth rejected causes one to become a womb for deception.

"From that time forth began Jesus to shew unto his disciples, how that he must go unto Jerusalem, and suffer many things of the elders and chief priests and scribes, and be killed, and be raised again the third day. Then Peter took him, and began to rebuke him, saying, Be it far from thee, Lord: this shall not be unto thee. But he turned, and said unto Peter, Get thee behind me, Satan: thou art an offence unto me: for thou savourest not the things that be of God, but those that be of men" (Matthew 16:21-23).

There's a couple of things I want to point out here. Jesus told Satan that he was an offense to him. Those who are offended in ministry are working directly with Satan. Notice I didn't say just a demon, I said Satan. Also I want to point out that Satan tried to offend (put a stumbling block) Jesus through Peter's fear. Fear is a gateway in which Satan can channel offense through an individual. Fearful people are easy to become offended too. Hear me in the spirit! Anything a person fears has the potential to offend them. When you fear change then change will offend you. When you fear authority then authority or anything authoritative will offend you. When you are afraid to trust people because of past hurts, you will become offended entering into relationship with anyone that you need to trust in order for the relationship to work. Offense keeps you from giving and receiving.

"And he went out from thence, and came into his own country; and his disciples follow him. And when the sabbath day was come, he began to teach in the synagogue: and many hearing him were astonished, saying, From whence hath this man these things? and what wisdom is this which is given unto him, that even such mighty works are wrought by his hands? Is not this the carpenter, the son of Mary, the brother of James, and Joses, and of Juda, and Simon? and are not his sisters here with us? And they were offended at him. But Jesus, said unto them, A prophet is not without honour, but in his own country, and among his own kin, and in his own house. And he could there do no mighty work, save that he laid his hands upon a few sick folk, and healed them. And he marvelled because of their unbelief. And he went round about the villages, teaching" (Mark 6:1-6).

First of all, if the method of a leader offends you, then you cannot receive from them. Also, I want to point out that familiarity causes offense. These people heard the wisdom coming out of Jesus' spirit and couldn't deny it. They also saw the mighty works God did through His hands, but they were offended at the fact that they knew Him and His family and they knew His history. They were offended at the fact that Jesus tried to teach them and because they were more "learned" or "seasoned" than Him, He should not have had anything to say to them. This caused them to dishonor Him therefore limiting the miraculous in their midst. Offended people are always the most dishonorable. The most dishonorable are the most powerless. This is why John the Baptist had a prophetic voice with no signs and wonders.

"Now when John had heard in the prison the works of Christ, he sent two of his disciples, And said unto him, Art thou he that should come, or do we look for another? Jesus answered and said unto them, Go and shew John again those things which ye do hear and see: The blind receive their sight, and the lame walk, the lepers are cleansed, and the deaf hear, the dead are raised up, and the poor have the gospel preached to them. And blessed is he, whosoever shall not be offended in me" (Matthew 11:2-6).John knew that Jesus was the Messiah, but he was offended because Jesus didn't come to his rescue when he was imprisoned. His offense kept him from his deliverance. This is a universal law that Jesus Himself couldn't violate. I'm pretty sure John felt unappreciated for paving the way for the Messiah to come. It also seems that John was was quickly and easily offended by Jesus, which proves that the offense started before Jesus' earthly ministry. This is why he never had any signs and wonders in his ministry. We're talking about a man who had the mantle of Elijah resting on his life! Since offense leads to dishonor and cancels out the supernatural, we can see why he didn't see the signs and wonders that Elijah did. You can have an inactive anointing or mantle upon your life because of offense and dishonor.

John the Baptist dishonored Jesus by reverting back to unbelief because he was offended that Jesus didn't come to his rescue. Even though he prepared the way for the Lord, he wasn't greater than the Lord. That same lordship he paved the way for, he also should have submitted too. But John knew Jesus every since they were little! Their mothers were close, they were related, and we can see how familiarity contributed to this offense and dishonor. Some people can get so familiar with you that they become offended by the authority of who you are. This is how John missed the fullness of his destiny. John was supposed to go further from where he stopped. Offense kept him in prison and honor would have gotten him out. It was also John's dishonor that got him in prison in the first place! John was put in prison by Herod because he told Herod it was not good that he took his brother's wife. You don't rebuke royalty! You don't see anywhere in scripture that Jesus rebuked Caesar, Herod, or Pontus Pilate directly. Offense will make you bitter and rebellious. The scriptures say that even the angels didn't bring accusation against leadership before God. "But chiefly them that walk after the flesh in the lust of uncleanness, and despise government. Presumptuous are they, selfwilled, they are not afraid to speak evil of dignities. Whereas angels, which are greater in power and might, bring not railing accusation against them before the Lord" (2 Peter 2:10-11).

If the angels are not able to speak against the dignitaries of the earth, then why do you think you're an exception? That's what's wrong with some prophets today... they think because they are prophets, they have the authority to challenge senior leadership. Senior leadership is in God's hands, not yours. Even if God gives a prophet a hard word for the leader, it will be only given to senior prophets who are mature. When Nathan gave a hard word to David, the prophet Nathan came with tact. He first touched David's heart by giving the parable concerning the sheep. He knew that even though He was God's prophet, his life was in the hand of the king. The king could still have his head (headship authority).

When submitting to a true process in God, you will begin to understand these things. We are in a kingdom and not a democracy where we pick our leadership and vote out what we don't agree with. As you read this... I plead with you. Do not allow pride and offense to rob you of your destiny! When you allow God to put you on the potters wheel and mold you, every area where pride is hidden and offense is possible will be exposed. Exposure is God's method of deliverance. Darkness cannot exists where light is present. You must come under the light of God's judgement and be purified by the fire of that light. Only then will you be perfect and complete in God. Ask Him for this! It may not feel good, but it's good for you. It will allow you to be eternally secure. God's methods are not to shame you, but to shame the devil and to make an open shame of him. Because of our fallen nature in Adam, it takes the measures mentioned in this book to strip you of the old man (Adam) and clothe you with the new man (Christ). Allowing God to judge your character during the process will deliver you from pride, offense, and the consequences of the two.

The Process

Lionel Blair, Sr

www.ingramcontent.com/pod-product-compliance
Lightning Source LLC
Chambersburg PA
CBHW030924090426
42737CB00007B/309

* 9 7 8 0 5 7 8 1 9 0 7 1 6 *